William Blake

Selected by
Peter Butter

PHOENIX

This edition first published in 2010

Phoenix edition first published in 2002

Typeset by Deltatype Ltd,
Birkenhead, Merseyside

Printed in Great Britain by
Clays Ltd, St Ives plc

A CIP catalogue reference for this book is
available from the British Library.

The Orion Publishing Group
Orion House
5 Upper St Martin's Lane
London
WC2H 9EA

Contents

Songs of Experience

William Blake

from Poetical Sketches

To The Evening Star

Thou fair-hair'd angel of the evening,
Now, whilst the sun rests on the mountains, light
Thy bright torch of love; thy radiant crown
Put on, and smile upon our evening bed!
Smile on our loves, and while thou drawest the
Blue curtains of the sky, scatter thy silver dew
On every flower that shuts its sweet eyes
In timely sleep. Let thy west wind sleep on
The lake; speak silence with thy glimmering eyes,
And wash the dusk with silver. Soon, full soon,
Dost thou withdraw; then the wolf rages wide,
And the lion glares thro' the dun forest:
The fleeces of our flocks are cover'd with
Thy sacred dew: protect them with thine influence.

Song

How sweet I roam'd from field to field
  And tasted all the summer's pride,
Till I the prince of love beheld
  Who in the sunny beams did glide!

He shew'd me lilies for my hair,
  And blushing roses for my brow;
He led me through his gardens fair,
  Where all his golden pleasures grow.

With sweet May dews my wings were wet,
  And Phœbus fir'd my vocal rage;
He caught me in his silken net,
  And shut me in his golden cage.

He loves to sit and hear me sing,
  Then, laughing, sports and plays with me;
Then stretches out my golden wing,
  And mocks my loss of liberty.

Song

My silks and fine array,
  My smiles and languish'd air,
By love are driv'n away;
  And mournful lean Despair
Brings me yew to deck my grave:
Such end true lovers have.

His face is fair as heav'n
  When springing buds unfold;
O why to him was't giv'n,
  Whose heart is wintry cold?
His breast is love's all worship'd tomb,
Where all love's pilgrims come.

Bring me an axe and spade,
  Bring me a winding sheet;
When I my grave have made
  Let winds and tempests beat:
Then down I'll lie, as cold as clay.
True love doth pass away!

Song

Love and harmony combine,
And around our souls intwine,
While thy branches mix with mine,
And our roots together join.

Joys upon our branches sit,
Chirping loud and singing sweet;
Like gentle streams beneath our feet
Innocence and virtue meet.

Thou the golden fruit dost bear,
I am clad in flowers fair;
Thy sweet boughs perfume the air,
And the turtle buildeth there.

There she sits and feeds her young,
Sweet I hear her mournful song;
And thy lovely leaves among,
There is love: I hear his tongue.

There his charming nest doth lay,
There he sleeps the night away;
There he sports along the day,
And doth among our branches play.

Song

I love the jocund dance,
 The softly-breathing song,
Where innocent eyes do glance,
 And where lisps the maiden's tongue.

I love the laughing vale,
 I love the echoing hill,
Where mirth does never fail,
 And the jolly swain laughs his fill.

I love the pleasant cot,
 I love the innocent bow'r,
Where white and brown is our lot,
 Or fruit in the mid-day hour.

I love the oaken seat
 Beneath the oaken tree,
Where all the old villagers meet,
 And laugh our sports to see.

I love our neighbours all,
 But, Kitty, I better love thee;
And love them I ever shall;
 But thou art all to me.

Song

Memory, hither come,
  And tune your merry notes;
And, while upon the wind
  Your music floats,
I'll pore upon the stream,
Where sighing lovers dream,
And fish for fancies as they pass
Within the watery glass.

I'll drink of the clear stream,
  And hear the linnet's song;
And there I'll lie and dream
  The day along:
And, when night comes, I'll go
  To places fit for woe,
Walking along the darken'd valley
With silent Melancholy.

Mad Song

The wild winds weep,
  And the night is a-cold;
Come hither, Sleep,
  And my griefs infold:
But lo! the morning peeps
  Over the eastern steeps,
And the rustling birds of dawn
The earth do scorn.

Lo! to the vault
  Of paved heaven,
With sorrow fraught
  My notes are driven:
They strike the ear of night,
  Make weep the eyes of day;
They make mad the roaring winds,
  And with tempests play.

Like a fiend in a cloud
  With howling woe,
After night I do croud,
  And with night will go;
I turn my back to the east
From whence comforts have increas'd;
For light doth seize my brain
With frantic pain.

from There Is No Natural Religion

(b)

I. Man's perceptions are not bound by organs of perception; he perceives more than sense (tho' ever so acute) can discover.

II. Reason, or the ratio of all we have already known, is not the same that it shall be when we know more.

III. [*This proposition is missing.*]

IV. The bounded is loathed by its possessor. The same dull round, even of a universe, would soon become a mill with complicated wheels.

V. If the many become the same as the few when possess'd, More! More! is the cry of a mistaken soul; less than All cannot satisfy Man.

VI. If any could desire what he is incapable of possessing, despair must be his eternal lot.

VII. The desire of Man being Infinite, the possession is Infinite & himself Infinite.

Conclusion. If it were not for the Poetic or Prophetic Character the Philosophic & Experimental would soon be at the ratio of all things, & stand still, unable to do other than repeat the same dull round over again.

Application. He who sees the Infinite in all things sees God. He who sees the Ratio only sees himself only.

Therefore God becomes as we are, that we may be as he is.

Songs of Innocence and of Experience

Shewing the Two Contrary States of the Human Soul

Songs of Innocence

Introduction

Piping down the valleys wild,
Piping songs of pleasant glee,
On a cloud I saw a child,
And he laughing said to me:

'Pipe a song about a Lamb.'
So I piped with merry chear.
'Piper, pipe that song again.'
So I piped, he wept to hear.

'Drop thy pipe, thy happy pipe,
Sing thy songs of happy chear.'
So I sung the same again,
While he wept with joy to hear.

'Piper, sit thee down and write
In a book that all may read.'
So he vanish'd from my sight.
And I pluck'd a hollow reed,

And I made a rural pen,
And I stain'd the water clear,
And I wrote my happy songs
Every child may joy to hear.

The Shepherd

How sweet is the Shepherd's sweet lot!
From the morn to the evening he strays;
He shall follow his sheep all the day
And his tongue shall be filled with praise.

For he hears the lamb's innocent call,
And he hears the ewe's tender reply;
He is watchful while they are in peace,
For they know when their Shepherd is nigh.

The Ecchoing Green

The Sun does arise,
And make happy the skies;
The merry bells ring
To welcome the Spring;
The sky-lark and thrush,
The birds of the bush,
Sing louder around
To the bells' chearful sound,
While our sports shall be seen
On the Ecchoing Green.

Old John with white hair
Does laugh away care,
Sitting under the oak
Among the old folk.
They laugh at our play,
And soon they all say:
'Such, such were the joys,
When we all, girls & boys,
In our youth-time were seen
On the Ecchoing Green.'

Till the little ones weary
No more can be merry;
The sun does descend,
And our sports have an end.
Round the laps of their mothers
Many sisters and brothers,
Like birds in their nest,
Are ready for rest;
And sport no more seen
On the darkening Green.

The Lamb

Little Lamb, who made thee?
Dost thou know who made thee?
Gave thee life & bid thee feed
By the stream & o'er the mead;
Gave thee clothing of delight,
Softest clothing, wooly, bright;
Gave thee such a tender voice,
Making all the vales rejoice?
  Little Lamb, who made thee?
  Dost thou know who made thee?

  Little Lamb, I'll tell thee,
  Little Lamb, I'll tell thee:
He is called by thy name,
For he calls himself a Lamb.
He is meek & he is mild,
He became a little child:
I a child & thou a lamb,
We are called by his name.
  Little Lamb, God bless thee.
  Little Lamb, God bless thee.

The Little Black Boy

My mother bore me in the southern wild,
And I am black, but O! my soul is white;
White as an angel is the English child,
But I am black, as if bereav'd of light.

My mother taught me underneath a tree,
And sitting down before the heat of day
She took me on her lap and kissed me,
And pointing to the east began to say:

'Look on the rising sun: there God does live,
And gives his light and gives his heat away;
And flowers and trees and beasts and men receive
Comfort in morning, joy in the noon day.

'And we are put on earth a little space,
That we may learn to bear the beams of love;
And these black bodies and this sun-burnt face
Is but a cloud, and like a shady grove.

'For when our souls have learn'd the heat to bear,
The cloud will vanish; we shall hear his voice,
Saying: "Come out from the grove, my love & care,
And round my golden tent like lambs rejoice." '

Thus did my mother say, and kissed me;
And thus I say to little English boy:
When I from black and he from white cloud free
And round the tent of God like lambs we joy,

I'll shade him from the heat, till he can bear
To lean in joy upon our father's knee;
And then I'll stand and stroke his silver hair,
And be like him, and he will then love me.

The Blossom

Merry, Merry Sparrow,
Under leaves so green,
A happy Blossom
Sees you swift as arrow
Seek your cradle narrow
Near my Bosom.

Pretty, Pretty Robin,
Under leaves so green,
A happy Blossom
Hears you sobbing, sobbing,
Pretty, Pretty Robin,
Near my Bosom.

The Chimney Sweeper

When my mother died I was very young,
And my father sold me while yet my tongue
Could scarcely cry "'weep! 'weep! 'weep! 'weep!'
So your chimneys I sweep, & in soot I sleep.

There's little Tom Dacre, who cried when his head,
That curl'd like a lamb's back, was shav'd; so I said,
'Hush, Tom, never mind it, for when your head's bare,
You know that the soot cannot spoil your white hair.'

And so he was quiet, & that very night,
As Tom was asleeping he had such a sight:
That thousands of sweepers, Dick, Joe, Ned & Jack,
Were all of them lock'd up in coffins of black;

And by came an Angel who had a bright key,
And he open'd the coffins & set them all free;
Then down a green plain leaping, laughing they run,
And wash in a river and shine in the Sun.

Then naked & white, all their bags left behind,
They rise upon clouds, and sport in the wind;
And the Angel told Tom, if he'd be a good boy,
He'd have God for his father & never want joy.

And so Tom awoke; and we rose in the dark,
And got with our bags & our brushes to work.
Tho' the morning was cold, Tom was happy & warm;
So if all do their duty, they need not fear harm.

The Little Boy Lost

'Father, father, where are you going?
O do not walk so fast.
Speak father, speak to your little boy,
Or else I shall be lost.'

The night was dark, no father was there;
The child was wet with dew;
The mire was deep, & the child did weep,
And away the vapour flew.

The Little Boy Found

The little boy lost in the lonely fen,
Led by the wand'ring light,
Began to cry, but God ever nigh
Appear'd like his father in white.

He kissed the child & by the hand led
And to his mother brought,
Who in sorrow pale, thro' the lonely dale,
Her little boy weeping sought.

Laughing Song

When the green woods laugh with the voice of joy,
And the dimpling stream runs laughing by,
When the air does laugh with our merry wit,
And the green hill laughs with the noise of it,

When the meadows laugh with lively green
And the grasshopper laughs in the merry scene,
When Mary and Susan and Emily
With their sweet round mouths sing 'Ha, Ha, He!'

When the painted birds laugh in the shade
Where our table with cherries and nuts is spread,
Come live & be merry and join with me,
To sing the sweet chorus of 'Ha, Ha, He!'

A Cradle Song

Sweet dreams, form a shade
O'er my lovely infant's head,
Sweet dreams of pleasant streams
By happy silent moony beams.

Sweet sleep, with soft down
Weave thy brows an infant crown.
Sweet sleep, Angel mild,
Hover o'er my happy child.

Sweet smiles, in the night
Hover over my delight.
Sweet smiles, Mother's smiles,
All the livelong night beguiles.

Sweet moans, dovelike sighs,
Chase not slumber from thy eyes.
Sweet moans, sweeter smiles,
All the dovelike moans beguiles.

Sleep, sleep, happy child.
All creation slept and smil'd.
Sleep, sleep, happy sleep,
While o'er thee thy mother weep.

Sweet babe, in thy face
Holy image I can trace.
Sweet babe, once like thee
Thy maker lay and wept for me,

Wept for me, for thee, for all,
When he was an infant small.
Thou his image ever see,
Heavenly face that smiles on thee,

Smiles on thee, on me, on all,
Who became an infant small.
Infant smiles are his own smiles;
Heaven & earth to peace beguiles.

The Divine Image

To Mercy, Pity, Peace and Love
All pray in their distress;
And to these virtues of delight
Return their thankfulness.

For Mercy, Pity, Peace and Love
Is God, our father dear,
And Mercy, Pity, Peace and Love
Is Man, his child and care.

For Mercy has a human heart,
Pity, a human face,
And Love, the human form divine,
And Peace, the human dress.

Then every man of every clime
That prays in his distress,
Prays to the human form divine:
Love, Mercy, Pity, Peace.

And all must love the human form
In heathen, turk or jew.
Where Mercy, Love & Pity dwell
There God is dwelling too.

Holy Thursday

'Twas on a Holy Thursday, their innocent faces clean,
The children walking two & two in red & blue &
  green;
Grey headed beadles walk'd before with wands as
  white as snow,
Till into the high dome of Paul's they like Thames'
  waters flow.

O what a multitude they seem'd, these flowers of
  London town!
Seated in companies they sit with radiance all their
  own.
The hum of multitudes was there, but multitudes of
  lambs,
Thousands of little boys & girls raising their innocent
  hands.

Now like a mighty wind they raise to heaven the voice
  of song,
Or like harmonious thunderings the seats of heaven
  among.
Beneath them sit the aged men, wise guardians of the
  poor.
Then cherish pity, lest you drive an angel from your
  door.

Night

The sun descending in the west,
The evening star does shine;
The birds are silent in their nest,
And I must seek for mine.
The moon, like a flower
In heaven's high bower,
With silent delight
Sits and smiles on the night.

Farewell, green fields and happy groves,
Where flocks have took delight;
Where lambs have nibbled, silent moves
The feet of angels bright;
Unseen they pour blessing,
And joy without ceasing,
On each bud and blossom
And each sleeping bosom.

They look in every thoughtless nest,
Where birds are cover'd warm;
They visit caves of every beast,
To keep them all from harm;
If they see any weeping
That should have been sleeping,
They pour sleep on their head
And sit down by their bed.

When wolves and tygers howl for prey,
They pitying stand and weep,
Seeking to drive their thirst away
And keep them from the sheep;
But if they rush dreadful,

The angels, most heedful,
Receive each mild spirit,
New worlds to inherit.

And there the lion's ruddy eyes
Shall flow with tears of gold,
And pitying the tender cries,
And walking round the fold,
Saying: 'Wrath by his meekness,
And by his health sickness,
Is driven away
From our immortal day.

'And now beside thee, bleating lamb,
I can lie down and sleep,
Or think on him who bore thy name,
Graze after thee and weep.
For, wash'd in life's river,
My bright mane for ever
Shall shine like the gold,
As I guard o'er the fold.'

Spring

Sound the Flute!
Now it's mute.
Birds delight
Day and Night;
Nightingale
In the dale,
Lark in Sky,
Merrily,
Merrily, Merrily to welcome in the Year.

Little Boy
Full of joy,
Little Girl
Sweet and small;
Cock does crow,
So do you;
Merry voice,
Infant noise,
Merrily, Merrily to welcome in the Year.

Little Lamb
Here I am;
Come and lick
My white neck,
Let me pull
Your soft Wool,
Let me kiss
Your soft face;
Merrily, Merrily we welcome in the Year.

Nurse's Song

When the voices of children are heard on the green
And laughing is heard on the hill,
My heart is at rest within my breast
And every thing else is still.

'Then come home, my children, the sun is gone down
And the dews of night arise;
Come, come, leave off play, and let us away
Till the morning appears in the skies.'

'No, no, let us play, for it is yet day
And we cannot go to sleep;
Besides, in the sky the little birds fly
And the hills are all cover'd with sheep.'

'Well, well, go & play till the light fades away
And then go home to bed.'
The little ones leaped & shouted & laugh'd
And all the hills ecchoed.

Infant Joy

'I have no name;
I am but two days old.'
What shall I call thee?
'I happy am,
Joy is my name.'
Sweet joy befall thee!

Pretty joy!
Sweet joy but two days old,
Sweet joy I call thee:
Thou dost smile,
I sing the while,
Sweet joy befall thee.

A Dream

Once a dream did weave a shade
O'er my Angel-guarded bed,
That an Emmet lost its way
Where on grass methought I lay.

Troubled, wilder'd and forlorn,
Dark, benighted, travel-worn,
Over many a tangled spray
All heart-broke I heard her say:

'O my children! do they cry?
Do they hear their father sigh?
Now they look abroad to see,
Now return and weep for me.'

Pitying, I drop'd a tear;
But I saw a glow-worm near,
Who replied: 'What wailing wight
Calls the watchman of the night?

'I am set to light the ground,
While the beetle goes his round:
Follow now the beetle's hum;
Little wanderer, hie thee home.'

On Another's Sorrow

Can I see another's woe,
And not be in sorrow too?
Can I see another's grief,
And not seek for kind relief?

Can I see a falling tear,
And not feel my sorrow's share?
Can a father see his child
Weep, nor be with sorrow fill'd?

Can a mother sit and hear
An infant groan, an infant fear?
No, no, never can it be,
Never, never can it be!

And can he who smiles on all
Hear the wren with sorrows small,
Hear the small bird's grief & care,
Hear the woes that infants bear,

And not sit beside the nest,
Pouring pity in their breast;
And not sit the cradle near,
Weeping tear on infant's tear;

And not sit both night & day,
Wiping all our tears away?
O, no, never can it be,
Never, never can it be!

He doth give his joy to all;
He becomes an infant small;
He becomes a man of woe;
He doth feel the sorrow too.

Think not thou canst sigh a sigh
And thy maker is not by;
Think not thou canst weep a tear
And thy maker is not near.

O, he gives to us his joy
That our grief he may destroy;
Till our grief is fled & gone
He doth sit by us and moan.

Songs of Experience

Introduction

Hear the voice of the Bard!
Who Present, Past, & Future sees,
Whose ears have heard
The Holy Word
That walk'd among the ancient trees,

Calling the lapsed Soul,
And weeping in the evening dew,
That might controll
The starry pole,
And fallen, fallen light renew!

'O Earth, O Earth return!
Arise from out the dewy grass;
Night is worn,
And the morn
Rises from the slumberous mass.

'Turn away no more.
Why wilt thou turn away?
The starry floor,
The wat'ry shore,
Is giv'n thee till the break of day.'

Earth's Answer

Earth rais'd up her head
From the darkness dread & drear.
Her light fled:
Stony dread!
And her locks cover'd with grey despair.

'Prison'd on wat'ry shore
Starry Jealousy does keep my den;
Cold and hoar,
Weeping o'er,
I hear the father of the ancient men.

'Selfish father of men!
Cruel, jealous, selfish fear!
Can delight,
Chain'd in night,
The virgins of youth and morning bear?

'Does spring hide its joy
When buds and blossoms grow?
Does the sower
Sow by night?
Or the plowman in darkness plow?

'Break this heavy chain
That does freeze my bones around.
Selfish! vain!
Eternal bane!
That free Love with bondage bound.'

The Clod and the Pebble

'Love seeketh not Itself to please,
Nor for itself hath any care,
But for another gives its ease,
And builds a Heaven in Hell's despair.'

So sang a little Clod of Clay
Trodden with the cattle's feet;
But a Pebble of the brook
Warbled out these metres meet:

'Love seeketh only Self to please,
To bind another to Its delight;
Joys in another's loss of ease,
And builds a Hell in Heaven's despite.'

Holy Thursday

Is this a holy thing to see
In a rich and fruitful land,
Babes reduc'd to misery,
Fed with cold and usurous hand?

Is that trembling cry a song?
Can it be a song of joy?
And so many children poor?
It is a land of poverty!

And their sun does never shine,
And their fields are bleak & bare,
And their ways are fill'd with thorns;
It is eternal winter there.

For where-e'r the sun does shine,
And where-e'r the rain does fall,
Babe can never hunger there,
Nor poverty the mind appall.

The Little Girl Lost

In futurity
I prophetic see
That the earth from sleep
(Grave the sentence deep)

Shall arise and seek
For her maker meek,
And the desart wild
Become a garden mild.

In the southern clime,
Where the summer's prime
Never fades away,
Lovely Lyca lay.

Seven summers old
Lovely Lyca told.
She had wander'd long,
Hearing wild birds' song.

'Sweet sleep, come to me
Underneath this tree.
Do father, mother, weep,
Where can Lyca sleep?

'Lost in desart wild
Is your little child.
How can Lyca sleep
If her mother weep?

'If her heart does ake,
Then let Lyca wake;
If my mother sleep,
Lyca shall not weep.

'Frowning, frowning night,
O'er this desart bright
Let thy moon arise,
While I close my eyes.'

Sleeping Lyca lay,
While the beasts of prey,
Come from caverns deep,
View'd the maid asleep.

The kingly lion stood
And the virgin view'd;
Then he gambol'd round
O'er the hallow'd ground.

Leopards, tygers play
Round her as she lay;
While the lion old
Bow'd his mane of gold,

And her bosom lick,
And upon her neck
From his eyes of flame
Ruby tears there came;

While the lioness
Loos'd her slender dress,
And naked they convey'd
To caves the sleeping maid.

The Little Girl Found

All the night in woe
Lyca's parents go
Over vallies deep,
While the desarts weep.

Tired and woe-begone,
Hoarse with making moan,
Arm in arm seven days
They trac'd the desart ways.

Seven nights they sleep
Among shadows deep,
And dream they see their child
Starv'd in desart wild.

Pale thro' pathless ways
The fancied image strays,
Famish'd, weeping, weak,
With hollow piteous shriek.

Rising from unrest,
The trembling woman prest
With feet of weary woe;
She could no further go.

In his arms he bore
Her, arm'd with sorrow sore,
Till before their way
A couching lion lay.

Turning back was vain;
Soon his heavy mane
Bore them to the ground;
Then he stalk'd around,

Smelling to his prey.
But their fears allay
When he licks their hands,
And silent by them stands.

They look upon his eyes
Fill'd with deep surprise,
And wondering behold
A Spirit arm'd in gold.

On his head a crown,
On his shoulders down
Flow'd his golden hair.
Gone was all their care.

'Follow me,' he said;
'Weep not for the maid;
In my palace deep
Lyca lies asleep.'

Then they followed
Where the vision led,
And saw their sleeping child
Among tygers wild.

To this day they dwell
In a lonely dell,
Nor fear the wolvish howl
Nor the lion's growl.

The Chimney Sweeper

A little black thing among the snow,
Crying "'weep! 'weep!' in notes of woe!
'Where are thy father & mother, say?'
'They are both gone up to the church to pray.

'Because I was happy upon the heath
And smil'd among the winter's snow,
They clothed me in the clothes of death,
And taught me to sing the notes of woe.

'And because I am happy & dance & sing,
They think they have done me no injury;
And are gone to praise God & his Priest & King,
Who make up a heaven of our misery.'

Nurse's Song

When the voices of children are heard on the green
And whisp'rings are in the dale,
The days of my youth rise fresh in my mind,
My face turns green and pale.

Then come home my children, the sun is gone down
And the dews of night arise;
Your spring & your day are wasted in play,
And your winter and night in disguise.

The Sick Rose

O Rose, thou art sick.
The invisible worm,
That flies in the night
In the howling storm,

Has found out thy bed
Of crimson joy;
And his dark secret love
Does thy life destroy.

The Fly

Little Fly,
Thy summer's play
My thoughtless hand
Has brush'd away.

Am not I
A fly like thee?
Or art not thou
A man like me?

For I dance
And drink & sing,
Till some blind hand
Shall brush my wing.

If thought is life
And strength & breath,
And the want
Of thought is death,

Then am I
A happy fly,
If I live
Or if I die.

The Angel

I Dreamt a Dream! what can it mean?
And that I was a maiden Queen,
Guarded by an Angel mild:
Witless woe was ne'er beguil'd!

And I wept both night and day,
And he wip'd my tears away,
And I wept both day and night,
And hid from him my heart's delight.

So he took his wings and fled;
Then the morn blush'd rosy red;
I dried my tears, & arm'd my fears
With ten thousand shields and spears.

Soon my Angel came again;
I was arm'd, he came in vain;
For the time of youth was fled
And grey hairs were on my head.

The Tyger

Tyger, Tyger, burning bright
In the forests of the night,
What immortal hand or eye
Could frame thy fearful symmetry?

In what distant deeps or skies
Burnt the fire of thine eyes?
On what wings dare he aspire?
What the hand dare seize the fire?

And what shoulder, & what art,
Could twist the sinews of thy heart?
And when thy heart began to beat,
What dread hand? & what dread feet?

What the hammer? what the chain?
In what furnace was thy brain?
What the anvil? what dread grasp
Dare its deadly terrors clasp?

When the stars threw down their spears
And water'd heaven with their tears,
Did he smile his work to see?
Did he who made the Lamb make thee?

Tyger, Tyger, burning bright
In the forests of the night,
What immortal hand or eye
Dare frame thy fearful symmetry?

My Pretty Rose Tree

A flower was offer'd to me,
Such a flower as May never bore;
But I said 'I've a Pretty Rose-tree,'
And I passed the sweet flower o'er.

Then I went to my Pretty Rose-tree,
To tend her by day and by night
But my Rose turn'd away with jealousy,
And her thorns were my only delight.

Ah! Sun-flower

Ah, Sun-flower! weary of time,
Who countest the steps of the Sun,
Seeking after that sweet golden clime
Where the traveller's journey is done;

Where the Youth pined away with desire,
And the pale Virgin shrouded in snow,
Arise from their graves and aspire
Where my Sun-flower wishes to go.

The Lilly

The modest Rose put forth a thorn,
The humble Sheep a threat'ning horn;
While the Lilly white shall in Love delight,
Nor a thorn nor a threat stain her beauty bright.

The Garden of Love

I went to the Garden of Love,
And saw what I never had seen:
A Chapel was built in the midst,
Where I used to play on the green.

And the gates of this Chapel were shut,
And 'Thou shalt not' writ over the door;
So I turn'd to the Garden of Love
That so many sweet flowers bore,

And I saw it was filled with graves,
And tomb-stones where flowers should be;
And Priests in black gowns were walking their rounds,
And binding with briars my joys & desires.

The Little Vagabond

Dear Mother, dear Mother, the Church is cold,
But the Ale-house is healthy & pleasant & warm;
Besides I can tell where I am used well,
Such usage in heaven will never do well.

But if at the Church they would give us some Ale,
And a pleasant fire our souls to regale,
We'd sing and we'd pray all the live-long day,
Nor ever once wish from the Church to stray.

Then the Parson might preach & drink & sing,
And we'd be as happy as birds in the spring;
And modest dame Lurch, who is always at Church,
Would not have bandy children nor fasting nor birch.

And God, like a father rejoicing to see
His children as pleasant and happy as he,
Would have no more quarrel with the Devil or the Barrel,
But kiss him & give him both drink and apparel.

London

I wander thro' each charter'd street
Near where the charter'd Thames does flow,
And mark in every face I meet
Marks of weakness, marks of woe.

In every cry of every Man,
In every Infant's cry of fear,
In every voice, in every ban,
The mind-forg'd manacles I hear:

How the Chimney-sweeper's cry
Every black'ning Church appalls,
And the hapless Soldier's sigh
Runs in blood down Palace walls;

But most thro' midnight streets I hear
How the youthful Harlot's curse
Blasts the new born Infant's tear,
And blights with plagues the Marriage hearse.

The Human Abstract

Pity would be no more
If we did not make somebody Poor;
And Mercy no more could be
If all were as happy as we;

And mutual fear brings peace,
Till the selfish loves increase.
Then Cruelty knits a snare
And spreads his baits with care.

He sits down with holy fears
And waters the ground with tears;
Then Humility takes its root
Underneath his foot.

Soon spreads the dismal shade
Of Mystery over his head,
And the Catterpiller and Fly
Feed on the Mystery;

And it bears the fruit of Deceit,
Ruddy and sweet to eat,
And the Raven his nest has made
In its thickest shade.

The Gods of the earth and sea
Sought thro' Nature to find this Tree;
But their search was all in vain:
There grows one in the Human Brain.

Infant Sorrow

My mother groan'd, my father wept;
Into the dangerous world I leapt,
Helpless, naked, piping loud,
Like a fiend hid in a cloud.

Struggling in my father's hands,
Striving against my swadling bands,
Bound and weary, I thought best
To sulk upon my mother's breast.

A Poison Tree

I was angry with my friend;
I told my wrath, my wrath did end.
I was angry with my foe;
I told it not, my wrath did grow.

And I water'd it in fears,
Night & morning with my tears;
And I sunned it with smiles,
And with soft deceitful wiles.

And it grew both day and night,
Till it bore an apple bright;
And my foe beheld it shine,
And he knew that it was mine,

And into my garden stole
When the night had veil'd the pole.
In the morning glad I see
My foe outstretch'd beneath the tree.

A Little Boy Lost

'Nought loves another as itself,
Nor venerates another so,
Nor is it possible to Thought
A greater than itself to know.

'And Father, how can I love you
Or any of my brothers more?
I love you like the little bird
That picks up crumbs around the door.'

The Priest sat by and heard the child;
In trembling zeal he seiz'd his hair;
He led him by his little coat;
And all admir'd the Priestly care.

And standing on the altar high,
'Lo, what a fiend is here!' said he,
'One who sets reason up for judge
Of our most holy Mystery.'

The weeping child could not be heard,
The weeping parents wept in vain;
They strip'd him to his little shirt,
And bound him in an iron chain;

And burn'd him in a holy place,
Where many had been burn'd before.
The weeping parents wept in vain.
Are such things done on Albion's shore?

A Little Girl Lost

Children of the future Age
Reading this indignant page,
Know that in a former time
Love! sweet Love! was thought a crime.

In the Age of Gold,
Free from winter's cold,
Youth and maiden bright
To the holy light,
Naked in the sunny beams delight.

Once a youthful pair,
Fill'd with softest care,
Met in garden bright,
Where the holy light
Had just remov'd the curtains of the night.

There in rising day,
On the grass they play;
Parents were afar,
Strangers came not near,
And the maiden soon forgot her fear.

Tired with kisses sweet,
They agree to meet
When the silent sleep
Waves o'er heaven's deep,
And the weary tired wanderers weep.

To her father white
Came the maiden bright;
But his loving look,
Like the holy book,
All her tender limbs with terror shook.

'Ona! pale and weak!
To thy father speak.
O the trembling fear!
O the dismal care!
That shakes the blossoms of my hoary hair.'

To Tirzah

Whate'er is Born of Mortal Birth
Must be consumed with the Earth
To rise from Generation free:
Then what have I to do with thee?

The Sexes sprung from Shame & Pride,
Blow'd in the morn, in evening died;
But Mercy chang'd Death into Sleep;
The Sexes rose to work & weep.

Thou Mother of my Mortal part
With cruelty didst mould my Heart,
And with false self-deceiving tears
Didst bind my Nostrils, Eyes & Ears;

Didst close my Tongue in senseless clay,
And me to Mortal Life betray.
The Death of Jesus set me free:
Then what have I to do with thee?

The School Boy

I love to rise in a summer morn,
When the birds sing on every tree;
The distant huntsman winds his horn,
And the sky-lark sings with me.
O! What sweet company.

But to go to school in a summer morn,
O! it drives all joy away;
Under a cruel eye outworn
The little ones spend the day
In sighing and dismay.

Ah! then at times I drooping sit,
And spend many an anxious hour;
Nor in my book can I take delight,
Nor sit in learning's bower,
Worn thro' with the dreary shower.

How can the bird that is born for joy
Sit in a cage and sing?
How can a child when fears annoy
But droop his tender wing,
And forget his youthful spring?

O! father & mother, if buds are nip'd
And blossoms blown away,
And if the tender plants are strip'd
Of their joy in the springing day
By sorrow and care's dismay,

How shall the summer arise in joy,
Or the summer fruits appear?
Or how shall we gather what griefs destroy,
Or bless the mellowing year
When the blasts of winter appear?

The Voice of the Ancient Bard

Youth of delight, come hither,
And see the opening morn,
Image of truth new born.
Doubt is fled, & clouds of reason,
Dark disputes & artful teazing.
Folly is an endless maze,
Tangled roots perplex her ways:
How many have fallen there!
They stumble all night over bones of the dead,
And feel they know not what but care,
And wish to lead others when they should be led.

A Divine Image

Cruelty has a Human Heart,
And Jealousy a Human Face;
Terror the Human Form Divine,
And Secrecy the Human Dress.

The Human Dress is forged Iron,
The Human Form a fiery Forge,
The Human Face a Furnace seal'd,
The Human Heart its hungry Gorge.

from Blake's Notebook

(c. 1791–3)

'Never pain to tell thy love'

Never pain to tell thy love,
Love that never told can be;
For the gentle wind does move
Silently, invisibly.

I told my love, I told my love,
I told her all my heart;
Trembling, cold, in ghastly fears –
Ah, she doth depart.

Soon as she was gone from me
A traveller came by
Silently, invisibly –
O, was no deny.

'I saw a chapel all of gold'

I saw a chapel all of gold
That none did dare to enter in;
And many weeping stood without,
Weeping, mourning, worshipping.

I saw a serpent rise between
The white pillars of the door,
And he forc'd & forc'd & forc'd –
Down the golden hinges tore,

And along the pavement sweet,
Set with pearls & rubies bright,
All his slimy length he drew,
Till upon the altar white

Vomiting his poison out
On the bread & on the wine.
So I turn'd into a sty
And laid me down among the swine.

'I asked a thief to steal me a peach'

I asked a thief to steal me a peach;
He turned up his eyes.
I ask'd a lithe lady to lie her down;
Holy & meek she cries.

As soon as I went
An angel came;
He wink'd at the thief
And smil'd at the dame,

And without one word said
Had a peach from the tree,
And still as a maid
Enjoy'd the lady.

A Cradle Song

Sleep, Sleep, beauty bright,
Dreaming o'er the joys of night.
Sleep, Sleep; in thy sleep
Little sorrows sit & weep.
Sweet Babe, in thy face
Soft desires I can trace,
Secret joys & secret smiles,
Little pretty infant wiles.

As thy softest limbs I feel,
Smiles as of the morning steal
O'er thy cheek, & o'er thy breast
Where thy little heart does rest.

O, the cunning wiles that creep
In thy little heart asleep!
When thy little heart does wake,
Then the dreadful lightnings break

From thy cheek & from thy eye,
O'er the youthful harvest nigh.
Infant wiles & infant smiles
Heaven & Earth of peace beguiles.

'Silent, Silent Night'

Silent, Silent Night,
Quench the holy light
Of thy torches bright;

For, possess'd of Day,
Thousand spirits stray
That sweet joys betray.

Why should joys be sweet
Used with deceit,
Nor with sorrows meet?

But an honest joy
Does itself destroy
For a harlot coy.

To Nobodaddy

Why art thou silent & invisible,
Father of Jealousy?
Why dost thou hide thyself in clouds
From every searching Eye?

Why darkness & obscurity
In all thy words & laws,
That none dare eat the fruit but from
The wily serpent's jaws?
Or is it because Secresy
Gains females' loud applause?

'Love to faults is always blind'

Love to faults is always blind,
Always is to joy inclin'd,
Lawless, wing'd & unconfin'd,
And breaks all chains from every mind.

Deceit to secresy confin'd,
Lawful, cautious & refin'd,
To every thing but interest blind,
And forges fetters for the mind.

Eternity

He who binds to himself a joy
Does the winged life destroy;
But he who kisses the joy as it flies
Lives in eternity's sun rise.

Riches

The countless gold of a merry heart,
The rubies & pearls of a loving eye,
The indolent never can bring to the mart,
Nor the secret hoard up in his treasury.

'The look of love alarms'

The look of love alarms
Because 'tis fill'd with fire;
But the look of soft deceit
Shall win the lover's hire.

The Book of Thel

I

PLATE 1

The daughters of Mne Seraphim led round their sunny flocks,
All but the youngest. She in paleness sought the secret air,
To fade away like morning beauty from her mortal day.
Down by the river of Adona her soft voice is heard,
And thus her gentle lamentation falls like morning dew:

'O life of this our spring! why fades the lotus of the water?
Why fade these children of the spring, born but to smile & fall?
Ah! Thel is like a wat'ry bow, and like a parting cloud,
Like a reflection in a glass, like shadows in the water,
Like dreams of infants, like a smile upon an infant's face,
Like the dove's voice, like transient day, like music in the air.
Ah! gentle may I lay me down and gentle rest my head,
And gentle sleep the sleep of death, and gentle hear the voice
Of him that walketh in the garden in the evening time.'

The Lilly of the Valley, breathing in the humble grass,
Answer'd the lovely maid, and said: 'I am a wat'ry weed,

And I am very small, and love to dwell in lowly vales;
So weak the gilded butterfly scarce perches on my head;
Yet I am visited from heaven, and he that smiles on all
Walks in the valley, and each morn over me spreads his hand,
Saying: "Rejoice, thou humble grass, thou new-born lilly flower,
Thou gentle maid of silent valleys and of modest brooks;
For thou shalt be clothed in light, and fed with morning manna,
Till summer's heat melts thee beside the fountains and the springs
To flourish in eternal vales." Then why should Thel complain?

PLATE 2

Why should the mistress of the vales of Har utter a sigh?'
She ceas'd & smil'd in tears, then sat down in her silver shrine.

Thel answer'd: 'O thou little virgin of the peaceful valley,
Giving to those that cannot crave, the voiceless, the o'erfired;
Thy breath doth nourish the innocent lamb, he smells thy milky garments,
He crops thy flowers while thou sittest smiling in his face,
Wiping his mild and meekin mouth from all contagious taints.

Thy wine doth purify the golden honey; thy perfume,
Which thou dost scatter on every little blade of grass
that springs,
Revives the milked cow, & tames the fire-breathing
steed.
But Thel is like a faint cloud kindled at the rising sun:
I vanish from my pearly throne, and who shall find my
place?'

'Queen of the vales,' the Lilly answer'd, 'ask the tender
cloud,
And it shall tell thee why it glitters in the morning
sky,
And why it scatters its bright beauty thro' the humid
air.
Descend, O little cloud, & hover before the eyes of
Thel.'

The Cloud descended, and the Lilly bow'd her modest
head,
And went to mind her numerous charge among the
verdant grass.

2

PLATE 3
'O little Cloud,' the virgin said, 'I charge thee tell to
me
Why thou complainest not when in one hour thou
fade away;
Then we shall seek thee, but not find. Ah! Thel is like
to thee:
I pass away; yet I complain, and no one hears my
voice.'

The Cloud then shew'd his golden head, & his bright form emerg'd,
Hovering and glittering on the air before the face of Thel:

'O virgin, know'st thou not? Our steeds drink of the golden springs
Where Luvah doth renew his horses. Look'st thou on my youth,
And fearest thou, because I vanish and am seen no more,
Nothing remains? O maid I tell thee, when I pass away
It is to tenfold life, to love, to peace, and raptures holy.
Unseen descending, weigh my light wings upon balmy flowers,
And court the fair eyed dew to take me to her shining tent.
The weeping virgin trembling kneels before the risen sun,
Till we arise link'd in a golden band and never part,
But walk united, bearing food to all our tender flowers.'

'Dost thou, O little Cloud? I fear that I am not like thee;
For I walk thro' the vales of Har, and smell the sweetest flowers,
But I feed not the little flowers. I hear the warbling birds,
But I feed not the warbling birds; they fly and seek their food.
But Thel delights in these no more, because I fade away;

And all shall say, "Without a use this shining woman
liv'd,
Or did she only live to be at death the food of
worms?" '

The Cloud reclin'd upon his airy throne and answer'd
thus:

'Then if thou art the food of worms, O virgin of the
skies,
How great thy use, how great thy blessing! Every thing
that lives
Lives not alone, nor for itself. Fear not, and I will call
The weak worm from its lowly bed, and thou shalt
hear its voice.
Come forth, worm of the silent valley, to thy pensive
queen.'

The helpless worm arose, and sat upon the Lilly's leaf,
And the bright Cloud sail'd on, to find his partner in
the vale.

3

PLATE 4
Then Thel astonish'd view'd the Worm upon its dewy
bed:
'Art thou a Worm? image of weakness, art thou but a
Worm?
I see thee like an infant wrapped in the Lilly's leaf.
Ah, weep not, little voice, thou canst not speak, but
thou canst weep.
Is this a Worm? I see thee lay helpless & naked,
weeping,

And none to answer, none to cherish thee with mother's smiles.'

The Clod of Clay heard the Worm's voice, & rais'd her pitying head;
She bow'd over the weeping infant, and her life exhal'd
In milky fondness; then on Thel she fix'd her humble eyes.

'O beauty of the vales of Har, we live not for ourselves.
Thou seest me the meanest thing, and so I am indeed;
My bosom of itself is cold, and of itself is dark,

PLATE 5
But he that loves the lowly pours his oil upon my head,
And kisses me, and binds his nuptial bands around my breast,
And says: "Thou mother of my children, I have loved thee,
And I have given thee a crown that none can take away."
But how this is, sweet maid, I know not, and I cannot know;
I ponder, and I cannot ponder; yet I live and love.'

The daughter of beauty wip'd her pitying tears with her white veil,
And said: 'Alas! I knew not this, and therefore did I weep.
That God would love a Worm I knew, and punish the evil foot

That wilful bruis'd its helpless form; but that he cherish'd it
With milk and oil I never knew, and therefore did I weep;
And I complain'd in the mild air, because I fade away,
And lay me down in thy cold bed, and leave my shining lot.'

'Queen of the vales,' the matron Clay answer'd, 'I heard thy sighs,
And all thy moans flew o'er my roof, but I have call'd them down.
Wilt thou, O Queen, enter my house? 'Tis given thee to enter
And to return; fear nothing; enter with thy virgin feet.'

4

PLATE 6

The eternal gates' terrific porter lifted the northern bar.
Thel enter'd in & saw the secrets of the land unknown.
She saw the couches of the dead, & where the fibrous roots
Of every heart on earth infixes deep its restless twists:
A land of sorrows & of tears where never smile was seen.

She wander'd in the land of clouds thro' valleys dark, list'ning
Dolours and lamentations; waiting oft beside a dewy grave
She stood in silence, list'ning to the voices of the ground,
Till to her own grave plot she came, & there she sat down,

And heard this voice of sorrow breathed from the hollow pit:

'Why cannot the Ear be closed to its own destruction?
Or the glist'ning Eye to the poison of a smile?
Why are Eyelids stor'd with arrows ready drawn,
Where a thousand fighting men in ambush lie?
Or an Eye of gifts & graces, show'ring fruits & coined gold?
Why a Tongue impress'd with honey from every wind?
Why an Ear a whirlpool fierce to draw creations in?
Why a Nostril wide inhaling terror, trembling & affright?
Why a tender curb upon the youthful burning boy?
Why a little curtain of flesh on the bed of our desire?'

The Virgin started from her seat, & with a shriek
Fled back unhinder'd till she came into the vales of Har.

Thel's motto

Does the Eagle know what is in the pit,
Or wilt thou go ask the Mole?
Can Wisdom be put in a silver rod,
Or Love in a golden bowl?

from The Marriage of Heaven and Hell

PLATE 3

As a new heaven is begun, and it is now thirty-three years since its advent, the Eternal Hell revives. And lo! Swedenborg is the Angel sitting at the tomb; his writings are the linen clothes folded up. Now is the dominion of Edom, & the return of Adam into Paradise; see Isaiah xxxiv & xxxv Chap.

Without Contraries is no progression. Attraction and Repulsion, Reason and Energy, Love and Hate, are necessary to Human existence.

From these contraries spring what the religious call Good & Evil. Good is the passive that obeys Reason. Evil is the active springing from Energy.

Good is Heaven. Evil is Hell.

The Voice of the Devil

PLATE 4

All Bibles or sacred codes have been the causes of the following Errors:

1. That Man has two real existing principles, Viz: a Body & a Soul.

2. That Energy, call'd Evil, is alone from the Body, & that Reason, call'd Good, is alone from the Soul.

3. That God will torment Man in Eternity for following his Energies.

But the following Contraries to these are True:

1. Man has no Body distinct from his Soul; for that call'd Body is a portion of Soul discern'd by the five Senses, the chief inlets of Soul in this age.

2. Energy is the only life and is from the Body, and Reason is the bound or outward circumference of Energy.

3. Energy is Eternal Delight.

PLATES 5–6

Those who restrain desire do so because theirs is weak enough to be restrained; and the restrainer or reason usurps its place & governs the unwilling.

And being restrain'd it by degrees becomes passive, till it is only the shadow of desire.

The history of this is written in Paradise Lost, & the Governor or Reason is call'd Messiah.

And the original Archangel, or possessor of the command of the heavenly host, is call'd the Devil or Satan, and his children are call'd Sin & Death.

But in the Book of Job Milton's Messiah is call'd Satan.

For this history has been adopted by both parties.

It indeed appear'd to Reason as if Desire was cast out; but the Devil's account is that the Messiah fell, & formed a heaven of what he stole from the Abyss.

This is shewn in the Gospel, where he prays to the Father to send the comforter, or Desire, that Reason may have Ideas to build on, the Jehovah of the Bible being no other than he who dwells in flaming fire. Know that after Christ's death, he became Jehovah.

But in Milton, the Father is Destiny, the Son a Ratio of the five senses, & the Holy-ghost Vacuum!

Note. The reason Milton wrote in fetters when he

wrote of Angels & God, and at liberty when of Devils & Hell, is because he was a true Poet and of the Devil's party without knowing it.

A Memorable Fancy

PLATES 6–7

As I was walking among the fires of hell, delighted with the enjoyments of Genius, which to Angels look like torment and insanity, I collected some of their Proverbs, thinking that as the sayings used in a nation mark its character, so the Proverbs of Hell shew the nature of Infernal wisdom better than any description of buildings or garments.

When I came home, on the abyss of the five senses, where a flat sided steep frowns over the present world, I saw a mighty Devil folded in black clouds hovering on the sides of the rock. With corroding fires he wrote the following sentence now perceived by the minds of men, & read by them on earth:

How do you know but ev'ry Bird that cuts the airy way
Is an immense world of delight, clos'd by your senses five?

Proverbs of Hell

PLATE 7

In seed time learn, in harvest teach, in winter enjoy.

Drive your cart and your plow over the bones of the dead.

The road of excess leads to the palace of wisdom.
Prudence is a rich ugly old maid courted by Incapacity.
He who desires but acts not breeds pestilence.
The cut worm forgives the plow.
Dip him in the river who loves water.
A fool sees not the same tree that a wise man sees.
He whose face gives no light shall never become a star.
Eternity is in love with the productions of time.
The busy bee has no time for sorrow.
The hours of folly are measur'd by the clock, but of wisdom no clock can measure.
All wholesome food is caught without a net or a trap.
Bring out number, weight & measure in a year of dearth.
No bird soars too high if he soars with his own wings.
A dead body revenges not injuries.
The most sublime act is to set another before you.
If the fool would persist in his folly he would become wise.
Folly is the cloke of knavery.
Shame is Pride's cloke.

PLATE 8

Prisons are built with stones of Law, Brothels with bricks of Religion.
The pride of the peacock is the glory of God.
The lust of the goat is the bounty of God.
The wrath of the lion is the wisdom of God.
The nakedness of woman is the work of God.
Excess of sorrow laughs. Excess of joy weeps.
The roaring of lions, the howling of wolves, the raging of the stormy sea, and the destructive sword are portions of eternity too great for the eye of man.
The fox condemns the trap, not himself.

Joys impregnate. Sorrows bring forth.
Let man wear the fell of the lion, woman the fleece of the sheep.
The bird a nest, the spider a web, man friendship.
The selfish smiling fool & the sullen frowning fool shall be both thought wise, that they may be a rod.
What is now proved was once only imagin'd.
The rat, the mouse, the fox, the rabbet watch the roots; the lion, the tyger, the horse, the elephant watch the fruits.
The cistern contains; the fountain overflows.
One thought fills immensity.
Always be ready to speak your mind, and a base man will avoid you.
Every thing possible to be believ'd is an image of truth.
The eagle never lost so much time as when he submitted to learn of the crow.

PLATE 9

The fox provides for himself, but God provides for the lion.
Think in the morning. Act in the noon. Eat in the evening. Sleep in the night.
He who has suffer'd you to impose on him knows you.
As the plow follows words, so God rewards prayers.
The tygers of wrath are wiser than the horses of instruction.
Expect poison from the standing water.
You never know what is enough unless you know what is more than enough.
Listen to the fool's reproach! it is a kingly title!

The eyes of fire, the nostrils of air, the mouth of
water, the beard of earth.
The weak in courage is strong in cunning.
The apple tree never asks the beech how he shall grow,
nor the lion the horse how he shall take his prey.
The thankful receiver bears a plentiful harvest.
If others had not been foolish, we should be so.
The soul of sweet delight can never be defil'd.
When thou seest an Eagle, thou seest a portion of
Genius; lift up thy head!
As the catterpiller chooses the fairest leaves to lay her
eggs on, so the priest lays his curse on the fairest
joys.
To create a little flower is the labour of ages.
Damn braces. Bless relaxes.
The best wine is the oldest, the best water the newest.
Prayers plow not! Praises reap not!
Joys laugh not! Sorrows weep not!

PLATE 10

The head Sublime, the heart Pathos, the genitals Beauty,
the hands & feet Proportion.
As the air to a bird or the sea to a fish, so is contempt
to the contemptible.
The crow wish'd every thing was black, the owl that
every thing was white.
Exuberance is Beauty.
If the lion was advised by the fox, he would be
cunning.
Improvement makes strait roads, but the crooked roads
without Improvement are roads of Genius.
Sooner murder an infant in its cradle than nurse
unacted desires.
Where man is not, nature is barren.

Truth can never be told so as to be understood and not be believ'd.

Enough! or Too much.

PLATE 11

The ancient Poets animated all sensible objects with Gods or Geniuses, calling them by the names and adorning them with the properties of woods, rivers, mountains, lakes, cities, nations, and whatever their enlarged & numerous senses could perceive.

And particularly they studied the genius of each city & country, placing it under its mental deity.

Till a system was formed, which some took advantage of & enslav'd the vulgar by attempting to realize or abstract the mental deities from their objects; thus began Priesthood,

Choosing forms of worship from poetic tales.

And at length they pronounc'd that the Gods had order'd such things.

Thus men forgot that All deities reside in the human breast.

*

PLATE 14

The ancient tradition that the world will be consumed in fire at the end of six thousand years is true, as I have heard from Hell.

For the cherub with his flaming sword is hereby commanded to leave his guard at tree of life; and when he does, the whole creation will be consumed and appear infinite and holy, whereas it now appears finite & corrupt.

This will come to pass by an improvement of sensual enjoyment.

But first the notion that man has a body distinct from his soul is to be expunged. This I shall do, by printing in the infernal method, by corrosives, which in Hell are salutary and medicinal, melting apparent surfaces away, and displaying the infinite which was hid.

If the doors of perception were cleansed, every thing would appear to man as it is, infinite.

For man has closed himself up, till he sees all things thro' narrow chinks of his cavern.

from Visions of the Daughters of Albion

PLATE 5

But when the morn arose, her lamentations renew'd.
The Daughters of Albion hear her woes, & eccho back
her sighs.

'O Urizen! Creator of men! mistaken Demon of heaven,
Thy joys are tears! thy labour vain to form men to
thine image.
How can one joy absorb another? are not different joys
Holy, eternal, infinite? and each joy is a Love.

'Does not the great mouth laugh at a gift? & the
narrow eyelids mock
At the labour that is above payment? and wilt thou
take the ape
For thy counsellor? or the dog for a schoolmaster to
thy children?
Does he who contemns poverty, and he who turns
with abhorrence
From usury, feel the same passion, or are they moved
alike?
How can the giver of gifts experience the delights of
the merchant?
How the industrious citizen the pains of the
husbandman?
How different far the fat fed hireling with hollow
drum,
Who buys whole corn fields into wastes, and sings
upon the heath:

How different their eye and ear! how different the
world to them!
With what sense does the parson claim the labour of
the farmer?
What are his nets & gins & traps, & how does he
surround him
With cold floods of abstraction, and with forests of
solitude,
To build him castles and high spires, where kings &
priests may dwell,
Till she who burns with youth and knows no fixed lot,
is bound
In spells of law to one she loaths? and must she drag
the chain
Of life in weary lust? must chilling murderous thoughts
obscure
The clear heaven of her eternal spring? to bear the
wintry rage
Of a harsh terror, driv'n to madness, bound to hold a
rod
Over her shrinking shoulders all the day, & all the
night
To turn the wheel of false desire, and longings that
wake her womb
To the abhorred birth of cherubs in the human form,
That live a pestilence & die a meteor & are no more;
Till the child dwell with one he hates, and do the deed
he loaths,
And the impure scourge force his seed into its unripe
birth
E'er yet his eyelids can behold the arrows of the day.

'Does the whale worship at thy footsteps as the hungry
dog?

Or does he scent the mountain prey, because his nostrils wide
Draw in the ocean? does his eye discern the flying cloud
As the raven's eye? or does he measure the expanse like the vulture?
Does thc still spider view the cliffs where eagles hide their young?
Or does the fly rejoice because the harvest is brought in?
Does not the eagle scorn the earth & despise the treasures beneath?
But the mole knoweth what is there, & the worm shall tell it thee.
Does not the worm erect a pillar in the mouldering church yard,

PLATE 6

And a palace of eternity in the jaws of the hungry grave?
Over his porch these words are written: "Take thy bliss, O Man!
And sweet shall be thy taste & sweet thy infant joys rcncw!" '

from America

A Prophecy

PLATE 6

'The morning comes, the night decays, the watchmen leave their stations;
The grave is burst, the spices shed, the linen wrapped up;
The bones of death, the cov'ring clay, the sinews shrunk & dry'd
Reviving shake, inspiring move, breathing! awakening!
Spring like redeemed captives when their bonds & bars are burst.
Let the slave grinding at the mill run out into the field,
Let him look up into the heavens & laugh in the bright air;
Let the inchained soul, shut up in darkness and in sighing,
Whose face has never seen a smile in thirty weary years,
Rise and look out; his chains are loose, his dungeon doors are open.
And let his wife and children return from the opressor's scourge;
They look behind at every step & believe it is a dream,
Singing: "The Sun has left his blackness, & has found a fresher morning,
And the fair Moon rejoices in the clear & cloudless night;
For Empire is no more, and now the Lion & Wolf shall cease." '

PLATE 7

In thunders ends the voice. Then Albion's Angel wrathful burnt
Beside the Stone of Night, and like the Eternal Lion's howl
In famine & war reply'd: 'Art thou not Orc, who serpent-form'd
Stands at the gate of Enitharmon to devour her children?
Blasphemous Demon, Antichrist, hater of Dignities,
Lover of wild rebellion, and transgressor of God's Law,
Why dost thou come to Angel's eyes in this terrific form?'

PLATE 8

The terror answer'd: 'I am Orc, wreath'd round the accursed tree.
The times are ended; shadows pass, the morning 'gins to break;
The fiery joy that Urizen perverted to ten commands,
What night he led the starry hosts thro' the wide wilderness,
That stony law I stamp to dust, and scatter religion abroad
To the four winds as a torn book, & none shall gather the leaves;
But they shall rot on desart sands, & consume in bottomless deeps,
To make the desarts blossom & the deeps shrink to their fountains,
And to renew the fiery joy, and burst the stony roof;
That pale religious letchery, seeking Virginity,
May find it in a harlot, and in coarse-clad honesty

The undefil'd, tho' ravish'd in her cradle night and
morn;
For every thing that lives is holy, life delights in life;
Because the soul of sweet delight can never be defil'd.
Fires inwrap the earthly globe, yet man is not
consum'd;
Amidst the lustful fires he walks; his feet become like
brass,
His knees and thighs like silver, & his breasts and head
like gold.'

from Europe

A Prophecy

PLATE 3

'Five windows light the cavern'd Man: thro' one he breathes the air;
Thro' one hears music of the spheres; thro' one the eternal vine
Flourishes, that he may receive the grapes; thro' one can look
And see small portions of the eternal world that ever groweth;
Thro' one himself pass out what time he please, but he will not;
For stolen joys are sweet, & bread eaten in secret pleasant.'

So sang a Fairy mocking as he sat on a streak'd Tulip,
Thinking none saw him; when he ceas'd I started from the trees,
And caught him in my hat as boys knock down a butterfly.
'How know you this,' said I, 'small Sir? where did you learn this song?'
Seeing himself in my possession, thus he answer'd me:
'My Master, I am yours; command me, for I must obey.'

'Then tell me what is the material world, and is it dead?'
He laughing answer'd: 'I will write a book on leaves of flowers,

If you will feed me on love-thoughts, & give me now
and then
A cup of sparkling poetic fancies. So, when I am tipsie,
I'll sing to you to this soft lute, and shew you all alive
The world, where every particle of dust breathes forth
its joy.'

from The Book of Urizen

PLATE 4
4. 'From the depths of dark solitude; from
The eternal abode in my holiness,
Hidden, set apart in my stern counsels
Reserv'd for the days of futurity,
I have sought for a joy without pain,
For a solid without fluctuation.
Why will you die, O Eternals?
Why live in unquenchable burnings? . . .

*

6. 'Here alone I, in books form'd of metals,
Have written the secrets of wisdom,
The secrets of dark contemplation,
By fightings and conflicts dire
With terrible monsters Sin-bred,
Which the bosoms of all inhabit,
Seven deadly Sins of the soul.

7. 'Lo! I unfold my darkness, and on
This rock place with strong hand the Book
Of eternal brass, written in my solitude:

8. 'Laws of peace, of love, of unity,
Of pity, compassion, forgiveness.
Let each chuse one habitation,
His ancient infinite mansion,
One command, one joy, one desire,
One curse, one weight, one measure,
One King, one God, one Law.'

*

4. He, in darkness clos'd, view'd all his race,
And his soul sicken'd! he curs'd
Both sons and daughters; for he saw
That no flesh nor spirit could keep
His iron laws one moment.

5. For he saw that life liv'd upon death.

PLATE 25
The Ox in the slaughter house moans,
The Dog at the wintry door.
And he wept & he called it Pity,
And his tears flowed down on the winds.

6. Cold he wander'd on high, over their cities,
In weeping & pain & woe;
And where-ever he wander'd in sorrows
Upon the aged heavens,
A cold shadow follow'd behind him
Like a spider's web, moist, cold & dim,
Drawing out from his sorrowing soul,
The dungeon-like heaven dividing,
Where ever the footsteps of Urizen
Walk'd over the cities in sorrow;

7. Till a Web, dark & cold, throughout all
The tormented element stretch'd
From the sorrows of Urizen's soul.
(And the Web is a Female in embrio.)
None could break the Web, no wings of fire,

8. So twisted the cords & so knotted
The meshes, twisted like to the human brain.

9. And all call'd it The Net of Religion.

from Letters

From *a* letter to Dr Trusler

dated 23 August 1799

Fun I love, but too much Fun is of all things the most loathsom. Mirth is better than Fun, & Happiness is better than Mirth. I feel that a Man may be happy in This World. And I know that This World Is a World of Imagination & Vision. I see Every thing I paint In This World, but Every body does not see alike. To the Eyes of a Miser a Guinea is more beautiful than the Sun, & a bag worn with the use of Money has more beautiful proportions than a Vine filled with Grapes. The tree which moves some to tears of joy is in the Eyes of others only a Green thing that stands in the way. Some See Nature all Ridicule & Deformity, & by these I shall not regulate my proportions; & Some Scarce See Nature at all. But to the Eyes of the Man of Imagination Nature is Imagination itself. As a man is, So he Sees. As the Eye is formed, such are its Powers. You certainly Mistake when you say that the Visions of Fancy are not to be found in This World. To Me This World is all One continued Vision of Fancy or Imagination, & I feel Flatter'd when I am told so. What is it sets Homer, Virgil & Milton in so high a rank of Art? Why is the Bible more Entertaining & Instructive than any other book? Is it not because they are addressed to the Imagination, which is Spiritual Sensation, & but mediately to the Understanding or Reason?

'To my Friend Butts I write'

To my Friend Butts I write
My first Vision of Light:
On the yellow sands sitting,
The Sun was Emitting
His Glorious beams
From Heaven's high Streams.
Over Sea, over Land
My eyes did Expand
Into regions of air
Away from all Care,
Into regions of fire
Remote from Desire.
The Light of the Morning
Heaven's Mountains adorning,
In particles bright
The jewels of Light
Distinct shone & clear.
Amaz'd & in fear
I each particle gazed,
Astonish'd, Amazed;
For each was a Man
Human-form'd. Swift I ran,
For they beckon'd to me,
Remote by the Sea,
Saying: 'Each grain of Sand,
Every stone on the Land,
Each rock & each hill,
Each fountain & rill,
Each herb & each tree,
Mountain, hill, earth & sea,
Cloud, Meteor & Star,
Are Men Seen Afar.'

I stood in the Streams
Of Heaven's bright beams
And Saw Felpham sweet
Beneath my bright feet
In soft Female charms;
And in her fair arms
My Shadow I knew,
And my wife's shadow too,
And My Sister & Friend.
We like Infants descend
In our Shadows on Earth,
Like a weak mortal birth.
My Eyes more & more
Like a Sea without Shore
Continue expanding,
The Heavens commanding,
Till the Jewels of Light,
Heavenly Men beaming bright,
Appear'd as One Man,
Who Complacent began
My limbs to infold
In his beams of bright gold;
Like dross purg'd away
All my mire & my clay.
Soft consum'd in delight
In his bosom Sun bright
I remain'd. Soft he smil'd,
And I heard his voice Mild,
Saying: 'This is My Fold,
O thou Ram horn'd with gold,
Who awakest from Sleep
On the Sides of the Deep.
On the Mountains around
The roarings resound

Of the lion & wolf,
The loud sea & deep gulf.
These are guards of My Fold,
O thou Ram horn'd with gold.'
And the voice faded mild.
I remain'd as a Child;
All I ever had known
Before me bright Shone.
I saw you & your wife
By the fountains of life.
Such the Vision to me
Appear'd on the Sea.

from Blake's Notebook

(c. 1802–4)

'Mock on, Mock on . . .'

Mock on, Mock on, Voltaire, Rousseau!
Mock on, Mock on – 'tis all in vain!
You throw the sand against the wind,
And the wind blows it back again.

And every sand becomes a Gem
Reflected in the beams divine;
Blown back they blind the mocking Eye,
But still in Israel's paths they shine.

The Atoms of Democritus
And Newton's Particles of Light
Are sands upon the Red sea shore,
Where Israel's tents do shine so bright.

from The Pickering MS

The Mental Traveller

I travel'd thro' a Land of Men,
A Land of Men & Women too,
And heard & saw such dreadful things
As cold Earth wanderers never knew.

For there the Babe is born in joy
That was begotten in dire woe,
Just as we Reap in joy the fruit
Which we in bitter tears did sow.

And if the Babe is born a Boy
He's given to a Woman Old,
Who nails him down upon a rock,
Catches his shrieks in cups of gold.

She binds iron thorns around his head,
She pierces both his hands & feet,
She cuts his heart out at his side
To make it feel both cold & heat.

Her fingers number every Nerve,
Just as a Miser counts his gold;
She lives upon his shrieks & cries,
And she grows young as he grows old,

Till he becomes a bleeding youth
And she becomes a Virgin bright;
Then he rends up his Manacles
And binds her down for his delight.

He plants himself in all her Nerves,
Just as a Husbandman his mould;
And she becomes his dwelling place
And Garden, fruitful seventy fold.

An Aged Shadow soon he fades,
Wand'ring round an Earthly Cot,
Full filled all with gems & gold
Which he by industry had got.

And these are the gems of the Human Soul:
The rubies & pearls of a lovesick eye,
The countless gold of the akeing heart,
The martyr's groan & the lover's sigh.

They are his meat, they are his drink;
He feeds the Beggar & the Poor
And the wayfaring Traveller;
For ever open is his door.

His grief is their eternal joy;
They make the roofs & walls to ring;
Till from the fire on the hearth
A little Female Babe does spring.

And she is all of solid fire
And gems & gold, that none his hand
Dares stretch to touch her Baby form,
Or wrap her in his swaddling-band.

But She comes to the man she loves,
If young or old, or rich or poor;
They soon drive out the aged Host,
A Beggar at another's door.

He wanders weeping far away
Untill some other take him in;
Oft blind & age-bent, sore distrest,
Untill he can a Maiden win.

And to allay his freezing Age
The Poor Man takes her in his arms;
The Cottage fades before his sight,
The Garden & its lovely Charms;

The Guests are scatter'd thro' the land,
For the Eye altering alters all;
The Senses roll themselves in fear,
And the flat Earth becomes a Ball;

The Stars, Sun, Moon, all shrink away –
A desart vast without a bound,
And nothing left to eat or drink,
And a dark desart all around.

The honey of her Infant lips,
The bread & wine of her sweet smile,
The wild game of her roving eye,
Does him to Infancy beguile.

For as he eats & drinks he grows
Younger & younger every day;
And on the desart wild they both
Wander in terror & dismay.

Like the wild Stag she flees away,
Her fear plants many a thicket wild;
While he pursues her night & day,
By various arts of Love beguil'd,

By various arts of Love & Hate;
Till the wide desart planted o'er
With Labyrinths of wayward Love,
Where roams the Lion, Wolf & Boar;

Till he becomes a wayward Babe,
And she a weeping Woman Old.
Then many a Lover wanders here,
The Sun & Stars are nearer roll'd,

The trees bring forth sweet Extacy
To all who in the desert roam,
Till many a City there is Built
And many a pleasant Shepherd's home.

But when they find the frowning Babe,
Terror strikes thro' the region wide;
They cry, 'the Babe! the Babe is Born!'
And flee away on every side.

For who dare touch the frowning form
His arm is wither'd to its root;
Lions, Boars, Wolves, all howling flee,
And every Tree does shed its fruit,

And none can touch that frowning form,
Except it be a Woman Old;
She nails him down upon the Rock,
And all is done as I have told.

The Land of Dreams

'Awake, awake! my little Boy,
Thou wast thy Mother's only joy.
Why dost thou weep in thy gentle sleep?
Awake! thy Father does thee keep.'

'O what Land is the Land of Dreams?
What are its Mountains & what are its Streams?
O Father, I saw my Mother there
Among the Lillies by waters fair.

'Among the Lambs clothed in white
She walk'd with her Thomas in sweet delight.
I wept for joy, like a dove I mourn;
O when shall I again return?'

'Dear Child, I also by pleasant Streams
Have wander'd all Night in the Land of Dreams;
But tho' calm & warm the Waters wide,
I could not get to the other side.'

'Father, O Father, what do we here
In this Land of unbelief & fear?
The Land of Dreams is better far
Above the Light of the Morning Star.'

The Crystal Cabinet

The Maiden caught me in the Wild,
Where I was dancing merrily;
She put me into her Cabinet,
And Lock'd me up with a golden Key.

This Cabinet is form'd of Gold
And Pearl & Crystal shining bright,
And within it opens into a World
And a little lovely Moony Night.

Another England there I saw,
Another London with its Tower,
Another Thames & other Hills,
And another pleasant Surrey Bower,

Another Maiden like herself,
Translucent, lovely, shining clear,
Threefold each in the other clos'd –
O, what a pleasant trembling fear!

O, what a smile! a threefold Smile
Fill'd me, that like a flame I burn'd.
I bent to Kiss the lovely Maid,
And found a Threefold Kiss return'd.

I strove to seize the inmost Form
With ardor fierce & hands of flame,
But burst the Crystal Cabinet
And like a Weeping Babe became,

A weeping Babe upon the wild,
And weeping Woman, pale, reclin'd;
And in the outward air again
I fill'd with woes the passing Wind.

Auguries of Innocence

To see a World in a Grain of Sand
And a Heaven in a Wild Flower,
Hold Infinity in the palm of your hand
And Eternity in an hour.

A Robin Red breast in a Cage
Puts all Heaven in a Rage.
A dove house fill'd with doves & Pigeons
Shudders Hell thro' all its regions.
A Dog starv'd at his Master's Gate
Predicts the ruin of the State.
A Horse misus'd upon the Road
Calls to Heaven for Human blood.
Each outcry of the hunted Hare
A fibre from the Brain does tear.
A Skylark wounded in the wing,
A Cherubim does cease to sing.
The Game Cock clip'd & arm'd for fight
Does the Rising Sun affright.
Every Wolf's & Lion's howl
Raises from Hell a Human Soul.
The wild deer wand'ring here & there
Keeps the Human Soul from Care.
The Lamb misus'd breeds Public strife,
And yet forgives the Butcher's Knife.
The Bat that flits at close of Eve
Has left the Brain that won't Believe.
The Owl that calls upon the Night
Speaks the Unbeliever's fright.
He who shall hurt the little Wren
Shall never be belov'd by Men.
He who the Ox to wrath has mov'd

Shall never be by Woman lov'd.
The wanton Boy that kills the Fly
Shall feel the Spider's enmity.
He who torments the Chafer's sprite
Weaves a Bower in endless Night.
The Catterpiller on the Leaf
Repeats to thee thy Mother's grief.
Kill not the Moth nor Butterfly,
For the last Judgment draweth nigh.
He who shall train the Horse to war
Shall never pass the Polar Bar.
The Beggar's Dog & Widow's Cat,
Feed them & thou wilt grow fat.
The Gnat that sings his Summer's song
Poison gets from Slander's tongue.
The poison of the Snake & Newt
Is the sweat of Envy's Foot.
The poison of the Honey Bee
Is the Artist's Jealousy.
The Prince's Robes & Beggar's Rags
Are Toadstools on the Miser's Bags.
A truth that's told with bad intent
Beats all the Lies you can invent.
It is right it should be so;
Man was made for Joy & Woe,
And when this we rightly know,
Thro' the World we safely go.
Joy & Woe are woven fine,
A Clothing for the Soul divine;
Under every grief & pine
Runs a joy with silken twine.
The Babe is more than swadling Bands;
Throughout all these Human Lands
Tools were made, & Born were hands –

Every Farmer Understands.
Every Tear from Every Eye
Becomes a Babe in Eternity;
This is caught by Females bright
And return'd to its own delight.
The Bleat, the Bark, Bellow & Roar
Are Waves that Beat on Heaven's Shore.
The Babe that weeps the Rod beneath
Writes 'Revenge' in realms of death.
The Beggar's Rags fluttering in Air
Does to Rags the Heavens tear.
The Soldier arm'd with Sword & Gun
Palsied strikes the Summer's Sun.
The poor Man's Farthing is worth more
Than all the Gold on Afric's Shore.
One Mite wrung from the Lab'rer's hands
Shall buy & sell the Miser's Lands;
Or if protected from on high
Does that whole Nation sell & buy.
He who mocks the Infant's Faith
Shall be mock'd in Age & Death.
He who shall teach the Child to Doubt
The rotting Grave shall ne'er get out.
He who respects the Infant's faith
Triumphs over Hell & Death.
The Child's toys & the Old Man's Reasons
Are the Fruits of the Two seasons.
The Questioner who sits so sly
Shall never know how to Reply.
He who replies to words of Doubt
Doth put the Light of Knowledge out.
The Strongest Poison ever known
Came from Cæsar's Laurel Crown.
Nought can deform the Human Race

Like to the Armour's iron brace.
When Gold & Gems adorn the Plow
To peaceful Arts shall Envy Bow.
A Riddle, or the Cricket's Cry,
Is to Doubt a fit Reply.
The Emmet's Inch & Eagle's Mile
Make Lame Philosophy to smile.
He who Doubts from what he sees
Will ne'er Believe, do what you Please.
If the Sun & Moon should doubt,
They'd immediately Go out.
To be in a Passion you Good may do,
But no Good if a Passion is in you.
The Whore & Gambler, by the State
Licenc'd, build that Nation's Fate.
The Harlot's cry from Street to Street
Shall weave Old England's winding Sheet.
The Winner's Shout, the Loser's Curse,
Dance before dead England's Hearse.
Every Night & every Morn
Some to Misery are Born.
Every Morn & every Night
Some are Born to sweet delight.
Some are Born to sweet delight,
Some are Born to Endless Night.
We are led to Believe a Lie
When we see not Thro' the Eye,
Which was Born in a Night to perish in a Night,
When the Soul Slept in Beams of Light.
God Appears & God is Light
To those poor Souls who dwell in Night,
But does a Human Form Display
To those who Dwell in Realms of Day.

from The Four Zoas

NIGHT 2

'What is the price of Experience? do men buy it for a song,
Or wisdom for a dance in the street? No, it is bought with the price
Of all that a man hath – his house, his wife, his children.
Wisdom is sold in the desolate market where none come to buy,
And in the wither'd field where the farmer plows for bread in vain.

'It is an easy thing to triumph in the summer's sun
And in the vintage, & to sing on the waggon loaded with corn;
It is an easy thing to talk of patience to the afflicted,
To speak the laws of prudence to the houseless wanderer,
To listen to the hungry raven's cry in wintry season,
When the red blood is fill'd with wine & with the marrow of lambs;
It is an easy thing to laugh at wrathful elements,
To hear the dog howl at the wintry door, the ox in the slaughter house moan,
To see a god on every wind, & a blessing on every blast,
To hear sounds of love in the thunderstorm that destroys our enemy's house,
To rejoice in the blight that covers his field, & the sickness that cuts off his children,
While our olive & vine sing & laugh round our door & our children bring fruit & flowers.

'Then the groan & the dolor are quite forgotten, & the slave grinding at the mill,
And the captive in chains, & the poor in the prison, & the soldier in the field
When the shatter'd bone hath laid him groaning among the happier dead.

'It is an easy thing to rejoice in the tents of prosperity;
Thus could I sing & thus rejoice, but it is not so with me!'

*

NIGHT 3

'Then Man ascended mourning into the splendors of his palace;
Above him rose a Shadow from his wearied intellect
Of living gold, pure, perfect, holy; in white linen pure he hover'd,
A sweet, entrancing self delusion, a wat'ry vision of Man,
Soft exulting in existence, all the Man absorbing.

'Man fell upon his face prostrate before the wat'ry shadow,
Saying, "O Lord, whence is this change? Thou knowest I am nothing."
And Vala trembled & cover'd her face, & her locks were spread on the pavement.

'I heard, astonish'd at the Vision, & my heart trembled within me;
I heard the voice of the Slumberous Man, and thus he spoke

Idolatrous to his own Shadow, words of Eternity uttering:
"O, I am nothing when I enter into judgment with thee.
If thou withdraw thy breath, I die & vanish into Hades;
If thou dost lay thine hand upon me, behold I am silent;
If thou withhold thine hand, I perish like a fallen leaf.
O, I am nothing, & to nothing must return again;
If thou withdraw thy breath, behold I am oblivion." '

*

NIGHT 7

And Urizen read in his book of brass in sounding tones:

'Listen, O Daughters, to my voice, Listen to the Words of Wisdom.
So shall you govern over all. Let Moral Duty tune your tongue,
But be your hearts harder than the nether millstone.
To bring the shadow of Enitharmon beneath our wondrous tree
That Los may Evaporate like smoke & be no more,
Draw down Enitharmon to the Spectre of Urthona
And let him have dominion over Los the terrible shade.
Compell the poor to live upon a Crust of bread by soft mild arts.
Smile when they frown, frown when they smile; & when a man looks pale
With labour & abstinence, say he looks healthy & happy;

And when his children sicken, let them die – there are enough
Born, even too many, & our Earth will be overrun
Without these arts. If you would make the poor live with temper,
With pomp give every crust of bread you give; with gracious cunning
Magnify small gifts; reduce a man to want a gift & then give with pomp.
Say he smiles if you hear him sigh. If pale, say he is ruddy.
Preach temperance: say he is overgorg'd & drowns his wit
In strong drink, tho' you know that bread & water are all
He can afford. Flatter his wife, pity his children, till we can
Reduce all to our will, as spaniels are taught with art.'

*

NIGHT 9

Urizen wept in the dark deep, anxious his Scaly form
To reassume the human; & he wept in the dark deep
Saying: 'O that I had never drank the wine nor eat the bread
Of dark mortality, nor cast my view into futurity, nor turn'd
My back dark'ning the present, clouding with a cloud,
And building arches high, & cities, turrets & towers and domes
Whose smoke destroy'd the pleasant gardens & whose running Kennels

Chok'd the bright rivers, burd'ning with my Ships the angry deep;
Thro' Chaos seeking for delight, & in spaces remote
Seeking the Eternal which is always present to the wise;
Seeking for pleasure which unsought falls round the infant's path
And on the fleeces of mild flocks who neither care nor labour.
But I, the labourer of ages, whose unwearied hands
Are thus deform'd with hardness, with the sword & with the spear
And with the Chisel & the mallet, I, whose labours vast
Order the nations, separating family by family,
Alone enjoy not. I alone, in misery supreme,
Ungratified give all my joy unto this Luvah & Vala.
Then Go, O dark futurity! I will cast thee forth from these
Heavens of my brain, nor will I look upon futurity more.
I cast futurity away, & turn my back upon that void
Which I have made; for lo, futurity is in this moment.
Let Orc consume, let Tharmas rage, let dark Urthona give
All strength to Los & Enitharmon, & let Los self-curs'd
Rend down this fabric, as a wall ruin'd & family extinct.
Rage, Orc! Rage, Tharmas! Urizen no longer curbs your rage.'

So Urizen spoke. He shook his snows from off his Shoulders & arose
As on a Pyramid of mist, his white robes scattering
The fleecy white; renew'd, he shook his aged mantles off

Into the fires. Then glorious, bright, Exulting in his
joy,
He sounding rose into the heavens in naked majesty,
In radiant Youth.

*

from Milton

Preface

PLATE 1
And did those feet in ancient time
Walk upon England's mountains green?
And was the holy Lamb of God
On England's pleasant pastures seen?

And did the Countenance Divine
Shine forth upon our clouded hills?
And was Jerusalem builded here
Among these dark Satanic Mills?

Bring me my Bow of burning gold;
Bring me my Arrows of desire;
Bring me my Spear; O clouds unfold!
Bring me my Chariot of fire!

I will not cease from Mental Fight,
Nor shall my Sword sleep in my hand,
Till we have built Jerusalem
In England's green & pleasant Land.

Would to God that all the Lord's people were Prophets.
Numbers XI.29

Book the first

PLATE 14
Then Milton rose up from the heavens of Albion
ardorous.

The whole Assembly wept prophetic, seeing in Milton's face
And in his lineaments divine the shades of Death & Ulro.
He took off the robe of the promise, & ungirded himself from the oath of God.

And Milton said: 'I go to Eternal Death! The Nations still
Follow after the detestable Gods of Priam, in pomp
Of warlike selfhood, contradicting and blaspheming.
When will the Resurrection come to deliver the sleeping body
From corruptibility? O when, Lord Jesus, wilt thou come?
Tarry no longer, for my soul lies at the gates of death.
I will arise and look forth for the morning of the grave;
I will go down to the sepulcher to see if morning breaks;
I will go down to self annihilation and eternal death,
Lest the Last Judgment come & find me unannihilate,
And I be seiz'd & giv'n into the hands of my own Selfhood.
The Lamb of God is seen thro' mists & shadows, hov'ring
Over the sepulchers in clouds of Jehovah & winds of Elohim,
A disk of blood, distant; & heav'ns & earth roll dark between.
What do I here before the Judgment? without my Emanation?
With the daughters of memory & not with the daughters of inspiration?

I in my Selfhood am that Satan; I am that Evil One!
He is my Spectre! In my obedience to loose him from my Hells,
To claim the Hells, my Furnaces, I go to Eternal Death.'

*

PLATE 22

. . . what time I bound my sandals
On to walk forward thro' Eternity, Los descended to me;
And Los behind me stood, a terrible flaming Sun, just close
Behind my back. I turned round in terror, and behold!
Los stood in that fierce glowing fire, & he also stoop'd down
And bound my sandals on in Udan-Adan. Trembling I stood
Exceedingly with fear & terror, standing in the Vale
Of Lambeth; but he kissed me, and wish'd me health,
And I became One Man with him arising in my strength.
'Twas too late now to recede. Los had enter'd into my soul;
His terrors now posses'd me whole! I arose in fury & strength.

'I am that Shadowy Prophet who Six Thousand Years ago
Fell from my station in the Eternal bosom. Six Thousand Years
Are finish'd. I return! both Time & Space obey my will.

I in Six Thousand Years walk up and down; for not one Moment
Of Time is lost, nor one Event of Space unpermanent,
But all remain; every fabric of Six Thousand Years
Remains permanent. Tho' on the Earth where Satan
Fell and was cut off all things vanish & are seen no more,
They vanish not from me & mine; we guard them first & last.
The generations of men run on in the tide of Time,
But leave their destin'd lineaments permanent for ever & ever.'

*

PLATE 24

Los is by mortals nam'd Time; Enitharmon is nam'd Space.
But they depict him bald & aged who is in eternal youth,
All powerful, and his locks flourish like the brows of morning.
He is the Spirit of Prophecy, the ever apparent Elias.
Time is the mercy of Eternity; without Time's swiftness,
Which is the swiftest of all things, all were eternal torment.
All the Gods of the Kingdoms of Earth labour in Los's Halls:
Every one is a fallen Son of the Spirit of Prophecy;
He is the Fourth Zoa, that stood around the Throne Divine.

*

PLATE 25

Thou seest the Constellations in the deep & wondrous Night;
They rise in order and continue their immortal courses
Upon the mountains & in vales, with harp & heavenly song,
With flute & clarion, with cups & measures fill'd with foaming wine.
Glitt'ring the streams reflect the Vision of beatitude,
And the calm Ocean joys beneath & smooths his awful waves.

PLATE 26

These are the Sons of Los, & these the Labourers of the Vintage.
Thou seest the gorgeous clothed Flies that dance & sport in summer
Upon the sunny brooks & meadows; every one the dance
Knows in its intricate mazes of delight artful to weave,
Each one to sound his instruments of music in the dance
To touch each other & recede, to cross & change & return.
These are the Children of Los. Thou seest the Trees on mountains;
The wind blows heavy, loud they thunder thro' the darksom sky,
Uttering prophecies & speaking instructive words to the sons
Of men. These are the Sons of Los, these the Visions of Eternity;
But we see only as it were the hem of their garments

When with our vegetable eyes we view these wondrous Visions.

*

PLATE 28

But others of the Sons of Los build Moments & Minutes & Hours
And Days & Months & Years & Ages & Periods, wondrous buildings;
And every Moment has a Couch of gold for soft repose,
(A Moment equals a pulsation of the artery),
And between every two Moments stands a Daughter of Beulah
To feed the Sleepers on their Couches with maternal care. . . .

Every Time less than a pulsation of the artery
Is equal in its period & value to Six Thousand Years;

PLATE 29

For in this Period the Poet's work is Done, and all the Great
Events of Time start forth & are conceiv'd in such a Period,
Within a Moment, a Pulsation of the Artery.

The Sky is an immortal Tent built by the Sons of Los;
And every Space that a Man views around his dwelling-place,
Standing on his own roof or in his garden on a mount
Of twenty-five cubits in height, such space is his Universe;

And on its verge the Sun rises & sets, the Clouds bow
To meet the flat Earth & the Sea in such an order'd
Space.
The Starry heavens reach no further, but here bend and
set
On all sides, & the two Poles turn on their valves of
gold;
And if he move his dwelling-place, his heavens also
move
Where'er he goes, & all his neighbourhood bewail his
loss.
Such are the Spaces called Earth, & such its dimension.
As to that false appearance which appears to the
reasoner,
As of a Globe rolling thro' Voidness, it is a delusion of
Ulro.
The Microscope knows not of this, nor the Telescope;
they alter
The ratio of the Spectator's Organs, but leave Objects
untouch'd.
For every Space larger than a red globule of Man's
blood
Is visionary, and is created by the Hammer of Los;
And every Space smaller than a Globule of Man's blood
opens
Into Eternity, of which this vegetable Earth is but a
shadow.
The red Globule is the unwearied Sun by Los created
To measure Time and Space to mortal Men every
morning.
Bowlahoola & Allamanda are placed on each side
Of that Pulsation & that Globule, terrible their power.

Book the Second

PLATE 31
Thou hearest the Nightingale begin the Song of Spring.
The Lark sitting upon his earthy bed, just as the morn
Apears, listens silent; then springing from the waving Cornfield loud
He leads the Choir of Day! trill, trill, trill, trill,
Mounting upon the wings of light into the great Expanse,
Reecchoing against the lovely blue & shining heavenly Shell.
His little throat labours with inspiration; every feather
On throat & breast & wings vibrates with the effluence Divine.
All Nature listens silent to him, & the awful Sun
Stands still upon the Mountain looking on this little Bird
With eyes of soft humility & wonder, love & awe.
Then loud from their green covert all the Birds begin their Song:
The Thrush, the Linnet & the Goldfinch, Robin & the Wren
Awake the Sun from his sweet reverie upon the Mountain;
The Nightingale again assays his song, & thro' the day
And thro' the night warbles luxuriant, every Bird of Song
Attending his loud harmony with admiration & love.
This is a Vision of the lamentation of Beulah over Ololon.

Thou perceivest the Flowers put forth their precious Odours,

And none can tell how from so small a center comes
 such sweets,
Forgetting that within that Center Eternity expands
Its ever during doors that Og & Anak fiercely guard.
First, e'er the morning breaks, joy opens in the flowery
 bosoms,
Joy even to tears, which the Sun rising dries; first the
 Wild Thyme
And Meadow-sweet, downy & soft, waving among the
 reeds,
Light springing on the air, lead the sweet Dance: they
 wake
The Honeysuckle sleeping on the Oak; the flaunting
 beauty
Revels along upon the wind; the White-thorn, lovely
 May,
Opens her many lovely eyes; listening the Rose still
 sleeps –
None dare to wake her; soon she bursts her crimson
 curtain'd bed
And comes forth in the majesty of beauty; every
 Flower,
The Pink, the Jessamine, the Wall-flower, the
 Carnation,
The Jonquil, the mild Lilly opes her heavens; every
 Tree
And Flower & Herb soon fill the air with an
 innumerable Dance,
Yet all in order sweet & lovely. Men are sick with
 Love.
Such is a Vision of the lamentation of Beulah over
 Ololon.

*

PLATE 32

'Distinguish therefore States from Individuals in those States.
States change, but Individual Identities never change nor cease . . .

Judge then of thy Own Self: thy Eternal Lineaments explore,
What is Eternal & what Changeable, & what Annihilable?
The Imagination is not a State: it is the Human Existence itself.
Affection or Love becomes a State when divided from Imagination.
The Memory is a State always, & the Reason is a State
Created to be Annihilated & a new Ratio Created.
Whatever can be Created can be Annihilated. Forms cannot.
The Oak is cut down by the Ax, the Lamb falls by the Knife;
But their Forms Eternal Exist For ever. Amen. Hallelujah!'

Thus they converse with the Dead, watching round the Couch of Death.
For God himself enters Death's Door always with those that enter,
And lays down in the Grave with them, in Visions of Eternity,
Till they awake & see Jesus, & the Linen Clothes lying
That the Females had Woven for them, & the Gates of their Father's House.

*

PLATE 40

But turning toward Ololon in terrible majesty, Milton
Replied: 'Obey thou the Words of the Inspired Man.
All that can be annihilated must be annihilated
That the Children of Jerusalem may be saved from slavery.
There is a Negation, & there is a Contrary;
The Negation must be destroy'd to redeem the Contraries.
The Negation is the Spectre, the Reasoning Power in Man.
This is a false Body, an Incrustation over my Immortal
Spirit, a Selfhood which must be put off & annihilated alway.
To cleanse the Face of my Spirit by Self-examination,

PLATE 41

To bathe in the Waters of Life, to wash off the Not Human,
I come in Self-annihilation & the grandeur of Inspiration;
To cast off Rational Demonstration by Faith in the Saviour,
To cast off the rotten rags of Memory by Inspiration,
To cast off Bacon, Locke & Newton from Albion's covering,
To take off his filthy garments, & clothe him with Imagination;
To cast aside from Poetry all that is not Inspiration,
That it no longer shall dare to mock with the aspersion of Madness
Cast on the Inspired by the tame high finisher of paltry Blots
Indefinite, or paltry Rhymes, or paltry Harmonies,

Who creeps into State Government like a catterpiller to destroy;
To cast off the idiot Questioner who is always questioning
But never capable of answering, who sits with a sly grin
Silent plotting when to question, like a thief in a cave;
Who publishes doubt & calls it knowledge, whose Science is Despair,
Whose pretence to knowledge is Envy, whose whole Science is
To destroy the wisdom of ages to gratify ravenous Envy,
That rages round him like a Wolf day & night without rest.
He smiles with condescension; he talks of Benevolence & Virtue;
And those who act with Benevolence & Virtue they murder time on time.
These are the destroyers of Jerusalem, these are the murderers
Of Jesus, who deny the Faith & mock at Eternal Life;
Who pretend to Poetry that they may destroy Imagination
By imitation of Nature's Images drawn from Remembrance.

from Jerusalem

PLATE 4

Of the Sleep of Ulro! and of the passage through
Eternal Death! and of the awaking to Eternal Life.

This theme calls me in sleep night after night, & ev'ry morn
Awakes me at sun-rise; then I see the Saviour over me
Spreading his beams of love & dictating the words of this mild song:

'Awake! awake, O sleeper of the land of shadows, wake! expand!
I am in you and you in me, mutual in love divine:
Fibres of love from man to man thro' Albion's pleasant land. . . .
I am not a God afar off, I am a brother and friend;
Within your bosoms I reside, and you reside in me.
Lo! we are One, forgiving all Evil, Not seeking recompense.
Ye are my members, O ye sleepers of Beulah, land of shades!'

But the perturbed Man away turns down the valleys dark:

'Phantom of the over heated brain! shadow of immortality!
Seeking to keep my soul a victim to thy Love! which binds
Man, the enemy of man, into deceitful friendships.
Jerusalem is not; her daughters are indefinite.
By demonstration man alone can live, and not by faith.'

*

PLATE 5

Trembling I sit day and night; my friends are astonish'd at me,
Yet they forgive my wanderings. I rest not from my great task!
To open the Eternal Worlds, to open the immortal Eyes
Of Man inwards into the Worlds of Thought, into Eternity
Ever expanding in the Bosom of God, the Human Imagination.
O Saviour pour upon me thy Spirit of meekness & love;
Annihilate the Selfhood in me, be thou all my life!

*

PLATE 31

He came down from Highgate thro' Hackney & Holloway towards London
Till he came to old Stratford, & thence to Stepney & the Isle
Of Leutha's Dogs, thence thro' the narrows of the River's side,
And saw every minute particular, the jewels of Albion, running down
The kennels of the streets & lanes as if they were abhorr'd.
Every Universal Form was become barren mountains of Moral
Virtue, and every Minute Particular harden'd into grains of sand,

And all the tendernesses of the soul cast forth as filth & mire,
Among the winding places of deep contemplation intricate,
To where the Tower of London frown'd dreadful over Jerusalem,
A building of Luvah, builded in Jerusalem's eastern gate to be
His secluded Court. Thence to Bethlehem, where was builded
Dens of despair in the house of bread; enquiring in vain
Of stones and rocks he took his way, for human form was none;
And thus he spoke, looking on Albion's City with many tears:

'What shall I do? what could I do, if I could find these Criminals?
I could not dare to take vengeance for all things are so constructed
And builded by the Divine hand that the sinner shall always escape,
And he who takes vengeance alone is the criminal of Providence.
If I should dare to lay my finger on a grain of sand
In way of vengeance, I punish the already punish'd. O whom
Should I pity if I pity not the sinner who is gone astray?
O Albion, if thou takest vengeance, if thou revengest thy wrongs,
Thou art for ever lost! What can I do to hinder the Sons

Of Albion from taking vengeance? or how shall I them
persswade?'

So spoke Los, travelling thro' darkness & horrid
solitude.
And he beheld Jerusalem in Westminster & Marybone
Among the ruins of the Temple, and Vala who is her
Shadow,
Jerusalem's Shadow bent northward over the Island
white.

*

PLATE 52

I saw a Monk of Charlemaine
Arise before my sight;
I talk'd with the Grey Monk as we stood
In beams of infernal light.

Gibbon arose with a lash of steel
And Voltaire with a wracking wheel;
The Schools, in clouds of learning roll'd,
Arose with War in iron & gold.

'Thou lazy Monk,' they sound afar,
'In vain condemning glorious War!
And in your Cell you shall ever dwell:
Rise, War, & bind him in his Cell!'

The blood red ran from the Grey Monk's side;
His hands & feet were wounded wide,
His body bent, his arms & knees
Like to the roots of ancient trees.

When Satan first the black bow bent
And the Moral Law from the Gospel rent,
He forg'd the Law into a Sword
And spill'd the blood of mercy's Lord.

Titus! Constantine! Charlemaine!
O Voltaire! Rousseau! Gibbon! Vain
Your Grecian Mocks and Roman Sword
Against this image of his Lord!

For a Tear is an Intellectual thing,
And a Sigh is the Sword of an Angel King,
And the bitter groan of a Martyr's woe
Is an Arrow from the Almightie's Bow.

*

PLATE 61

'Behold in the Visions of Elohim Jehovah, behold Joseph & Mary
And be comforted, O Jerusalem, in the Visions of Jehovah Elohim.'

She looked & saw Joseph the Carpenter in Nazareth, & Mary
His espoused Wife. And Mary said, 'If thou put me away from thee,
Dost thou not murder me?' Joseph spoke in anger & fury, 'Should I
Marry a Harlot & an Adulteress?' Mary answer'd, 'Art thou more pure
Than thy Maker who forgiveth Sins & calls again Her that is Lost?

Tho' She hates, he calls her again in love. I love my dear Joseph,
But he driveth me away from his presence; yet I hear the voice of God
In the voice of my Husband; tho' he is angry for a moment, he will not
Utterly cast me away. If I were pure, never could I taste the sweets
Of the Forgiveness of Sins; if I were holy, I never could behold the tears
Of love of him who loves me in the midst of his anger in furnace of fire.'

'Ah my Mary!' said Joseph, weeping over & embracing her closely in
His arms, 'Doth he forgive Jerusalem, & not exact Purity from her who is
Polluted? I heard his voice in my sleep & his Angel in my dream,
Saying, "Doth Jehovah Forgive a Debt only on condition that it shall
Be Payed? Doth he Forgive Pollution only on conditions of Purity?
That Debt is not Forgiven! That Pollution is not Forgiven!
Such is the Forgiveness of the Gods, the Moral Virtues of the
Heathen, whose tender Mercies are Cruelty. But Jehovah's Salvation
Is without Money & without Price, in the Continual Forgiveness of Sins,
In the Perpetual Mutual Sacrifice in Great Eternity. For behold,

There is none that liveth & Sinneth not! And this is the Covenant
Of Jehovah: If you Forgive one-another, so shall Jehovah Forgive You,
That He Himself may Dwell among You. Fear not then to take
To thee Mary thy Wife, for she is with Child by the Holy Ghost." '

*

PLATE 65
Then left the Sons of Urizen the plow & harrow, the loom,
The hammer & the chisel & the rule & compasses; from London fleeing,
They forg'd the sword on Cheviot, the chariot of war & the battle-ax,
The trumpet fitted to mortal battle, & the flute of summer in Annandale.
And all the Arts of Life they chang'd into the Arts of Death in Albion:
The hour-glass contemn'd because its simple workmanship
Was like the workmanship of the plowman, & the water wheel
That raises water into cisterns broken & burn'd with fire
Because its workmanship was like the workmanship of the shepherd.
And in their stead, intricate wheels invented, wheel without wheel,
To perplex youth in their outgoings & to bind to labours in Albion

Of day & night the myriads of eternity; that they may grind
And polish brass & iron hour after hour, laborious task,
Kept ignorant of its use; that they might spend the days of wisdom
In sorrowful drudgery to obtain a scanty pittance of bread;
In ignorance to view a small portion & think that All,
And call it Demonstration, blind to all the simple rules of life.

*

PLATE 91

'He who would see the Divinity must see him in his Children:
One first, in friendship & love, then a Divine Family, & in the midst
Jesus will appear; so he who wishes to see a Vision, a perfect Whole,
Must see it in its Minute Particulars, Organized, & not as thou,
O Fiend of Righteousness, pretendest; thine is a Disorganized
And snowy cloud, brooder of tempests & destructive War.
You smile with pomp & rigor, you talk of benevolence & virtue;
I act with benevolence & Virtue & get murder'd time after time.
You accumulate Particulars & murder by analyzing, that you
May take the aggregate; & you call the aggregate Moral Law;

And you call that swell'd & bloated Form a Minute
Particular.
But General Forms have their vitality in Particulars; &
every
Particular is a Man, a Divine Member of the Divine
Jesus.'

So Los cried at his Anvil, in the horrible darkness
weeping. . . .

PLATE 96

Then Jesus appeared standing by Albion as the Good
Shepherd
By the lost Sheep that he hath found, & Albion knew
that it
Was the Lord, the Universal Humanity; & Albion saw
his Form
A Man, & they conversed as Man with Man in Ages of
Eternity.
And the Divine Appearance was the likeness &
similitude of Los.

Albion said: 'O Lord, what can I do? my Selfhood cruel
Marches against thee, deceitful, from Sinai & from
Edom
Into the Wilderness of Judah, to meet thee in his pride.
I behold the Visions of my deadly Sleep of Six
Thousand Years
Dazling around thy skirts like a Serpent of precious
stones & gold.
I know it is my Self, O my Divine Creator &
Redeemer.'

Jesus replied: 'Fear not, Albion; unless I die thou canst not live,
But if I die I shall arise again & thou with me.
This is Friendship & Brotherhood; without it Man Is Not.'

So Jesus spoke. The Covering Cherub coming on in darkness
Overshadow'd them, & Jesus said: 'Thus do Men in Eternity,
One for another to put off by forgiveness every sin.'

Albion reply'd: 'Cannot Man exist without Mysterious
Offering of Self for Another? is this Friendship & Brotherhood?
I see thee in the likeness & similitude of Los my Friend.'

Jesus said: 'Wouldst thou love one who never died
For thee, or ever die for one who had not died for thee?
And if God dieth not for Man & giveth not himself
Eternally for Man, Man could not exist; for Man is Love,
As God is Love. Every kindness to another is a little Death
In the Divine Image, nor can Man exist but by Brotherhood.'

So saying, the Cloud overshadowing divided them asunder.
Albion stood in terror, not for himself but for his Friend
Divine, & Self was lost in the contemplation of faith

And wonder at the Divine Mercy & at Los's sublime honour.

'Do I sleep amidst danger to Friends? O my Cities & Counties,
Do you sleep? Rouze up, rouze up! Eternal Death is abroad!'

So Albion spoke, & threw himself into the Furnaces of affliction.
All was a Vision, all a Dream! The Furnaces became
Fountains of Living Waters flowing from the Humanity Divine.
And all the Cities of Albion rose from their Slumbers, and All
The Sons & Daughters of Albion on soft clouds, Waking from Sleep.
Soon all around remote the Heavens burnt with flaming fires,
And Urizen & Luvah & Tharmas & Urthona arose into
Albion's Bosom. Then Albion stood before Jesus in the Clouds
Of Heaven, Fourfold among the Visions of God in Eternity:

PLATE 97
'Awake, Awake, Jerusalem! O lovely Emanation of Albion,
Awake and overspread all Nations as in Ancient Time;
For lo! the Night of Death is past and the Eternal Day
Appears upon our Hills! Awake, Jerusalem, and come away!'

from For the Sexes: The Gates of Paradise

The Gates of Paradise

Mutual Forgiveness of each Vice,
Such are the Gates of Paradise.
Against the Accuser's chief desire
Who walk'd among the Stones of Fire
Jehovah's Finger Wrote the Law;
Then Wept, then rose in Zeal & Awe
And the Dead Corpse from Sinai's heat
Buried beneath his Mercy Seat.
O Christians, Christians, tell me Why
You rear it on your Altars high.

To the Accuser Who Is the God of This World

Truly, My Satan, thou art but a Dunce,
And dost not know the Garment from the Man.
Every Harlot was a Virgin once,
Nor canst thou ever change Kate into Nan.

Tho' thou art Worship'd by the Names Divine
Of Jesus & Jehovah, thou art still
The Son of Morn in weary Night's decline,
The lost Traveller's Dream under the Hill.

Chronology of Blake's Life

Year	*Age*	*Life*
1757		Born 28 November, son of James Blake, hosier, in London
1765–7	8–10	Sees angels in a tree
1768–72	10–14	Attends Henry Pars's drawing school
1772–9	14–21	Apprenticed to James Basire engraver; makes drawings of monuments in Westminster Abbey
1779	21	Student at Royal Academy; exhibits there in 1780. Making living as engraver
1782	24	Marries Catherine Boucher (b. 1762) No children
1783	26	*Poetical Sketches* printed
1784	26	Death of father. Sets up print shop with fellow Basire apprentice James Parker
1784–5	26–7	*Island in the Moon* written, not published
1788	30	First works in illuminated printing – *All Religions Are One* and *There Is No Natural Religion*
1789	31	*Tiriel* written, not published; *Songs of Innocence* and *Thel* etched
1790–?93	32–5	*Marriage of Heaven and Hell*
1791	33	*The French Revolution* printed, not published
1793	35	*For Children: The Gates of Paradise, Visions of the Daughters of Albion, America, Songs of Experience* advertised for sale
1794	36	*Europe* and *Book of Urizen* *Songs of Innocence and of Experience* brought together

Chronology of his Times

Year	Artistic Context	Historical Events
1760	MacPherson, first 'Ossian' poems	Wedgwood's pottery founded
1765	Percy, *Reliques of Ancient Poetry*	
1769		Arkwright's first spinning mill
1770	Birth of Wordsworth	
1774–83		Development of Watt's steam engine
1775–83		American Revolution
1779–81	Johnson, *Lives of the Poets*	
1780		Gordon Riots in London; attack on Newgate prison seen by Blake
1783	Crabbe, *The Village*	
1785	Cowper, *The Task*	
1786	Burns, *Poems Chiefly in the Scottish Dialect*	
1788	Birth of Byron	
1789		French Revolution
1791	E. Darwin, *Botanic Garden* with engravings by Blake	September massacres in France
1791–2	Paine, *Rights of Man*	
1792	Wollstonecraft, *A Vindication of the Rights of Woman*	Invasion of France by Austria, Prussia defeated
1793	Godwin, *Inquiry Concerning Political Justice*	King Louis executed; Reign of Terror England at war with France
1794		Pitt Prime Minister
1794–5		Robespierre executed

Year	Age	Life
1795	37	*Song of Los*, *Book of Los* and *Book of Ahania*
1795–7	37–9	Draws copious illustrations to Young's *Night Thoughts*
1797	39	Begins *Vala*, later titled *The Four Zoas*
1799	41	Makes pictures for Thomas Butts
1800–3	42–5	Works on projects for William Hayley, on illustrations to Milton's *Comus*, on *Vala* and probably *Milton*; learns Greek, Latin and Hebrew
1803	45	Fracas with a soldier, leading to trial for sedition; acquitted 1804
1804	46	Title pages of *Milton* and *Jerusalem* etched; *The Four Zoas* eventually (?1807) abandoned
1805	47	Makes designs for Blair's *The Grave*; water colour illustrations to Gray's *Poems* completed
1809	51	Unsuccessful exhibition of his paintings. For next decade suffers poverty and neglect
1818	60	Meets John Linnell and John Varley
1820	62	Makes woodcuts for an edition of Virgil's *Pastorals*.
1822–5	64–7	*The Ghost of Abel* etched and illustrations of the Book of Job
1824–7	66–9	Meets Samuel Palmer and becomes inspirer of group of young artists, the 'Ancients'. Makes illustrations to Bunyan's *Pilgrim's Progress* and Dante's *Divine Comedy*
1827	69	Dies 12 August

Year	Artistic Context	Historical Events
1795	Birth of Keats	Napoleon commander in Italy
1798	Wordsworth and Coleridge, *Lyrical Ballads*	
1799		Napoleon First Consul
1803		Resumption of war with France
1804		Napoleon Emperor
1805		Battle of Trafalgar
1808	Beethoven, Fifth Symphony	
1809–13		Wellington's successful campaigns against France in Spain and Portugal
1811	Jane Austen, *Sense and Sensibility*	
1815		Napoleon's final defeat at Waterloo
1817	Keats, *Endymion*; other poems 1817–20	
1819		'Peterloo' massacre
1820–21		Revolutionary outbreaks in Spain, Portugal, Piedmont, Greece
1823	Constable, 'Hay Wain'	
1824	Death of Byron	
1825	Hazlitt, *The Spirit of the Age*	Stockton to Darlington railway line opened